THE
Weekly
Word

THE
Weekly
Word

*In Depth Bible Studies taken from
the Jewish Weekly Torah Portion*

Rabbi Pesach Wolicki

Table of Contents

Genesis

Bereishit

Genesis 1:1-6:8

The Creation of Responsibility

M Y WIFE AND I were introduced by a mutual friend, a neighbor of mine in Jerusalem. I was sure I would marry her from the moment we met. We were engaged less than a week later and married soon thereafter.

How did I know she was the one? That's a question I'm not sure I can answer. Most people are not so sure. Maybe that's why one of the traditional Jewish blessings that we bestow on a bride and groom is that God should make them as happy as "His creations in the garden of Eden." To state the obvious, no two people in history were ever so sure they had found the right spouse as Adam and Eve. I mean, what were the options?

This leads us to a perplexing sequence of verses in the Bible portion of Bereishit, which describe the union of Adam and Eve (Genesis 2:18-20):

Then the Lord God said, "It is not good that the man should be alone; I will make him a helper fit for him."

Now, out of the ground, the Lord God had formed every beast of the field and every bird of the heavens and brought them to the man to see what he would call them. And whatever the man called every living creature, that was its name.

The man gave names to all livestock to the birds of the heavens, and to every beast of the field. But for Adam there was not found a helper fit for him.

To sum up, the sequence of events is as follows:

(18) It's not good for man to be alone, let's find him a mate.
(19) God brings Adam all the animals to name.
(20) Adam names the animals and does not find a mate.

Based on the order of the verses, it seems like naming the animals was part of the process of finding Abraham a soulmate. It almost seems as if Adam was "dating" and checking out his options. "Adam, let's find you a wife. How about the elephant? Nope. Squirrel? Nah…"

What does naming all the animals have to do with finding a wife?

While this sequence is often overlooked, it teaches a powerful lesson. Simply put, Man is not an animal. By naming the animals Adam declared them to be *others*, outside of him. In naming them he also declares his primacy over them. Superiors name subordinates, subordinates do not name their superiors. Through this process, Adam came to realize that he has no partnership with the animal kingdom. In the words of the text "But for Adam there was not found a helper fit for him."

There is no *marriage* in the animal kingdom. There is *mating*, for sure, but not marriage. Animals bear no responsibility. They have no task. Animals are bodies without souls. It is specifically man's search for a partner in responsibility and mission that brings him to the realization that he is not a member of the animal kingdom. He *has* a body but that is not who he is. He *is* a soul.

Once Man realizes that he is not an animal, he is ready for his true partner and mate. Through his search, Adam discovered that he was alone. Only then was he ready to feel whole, to be completed by the woman.

A few verses before this sequence, Adam was given his mission by God:

The Lord God took the man and put him in the garden of Eden to work it and protect it. (Genesis 2:15).

To work and to protect. Notice that the verse does not say "to enjoy and to express himself." It does not say "to indulge in pleasures and to be free." "To work" means, simply, that there is work to be done. I have to act, to be productive, to make things better. "To protect" means that I must do no harm; that I must protect God's creation.

To work, to protect.... in other words, we are on this earth *to be responsible.* To be responsible means that my life is not about me. To be responsible means that I am accountable, it means that I have a calling and a mission. This is man's covenantal responsibility to his creator.

As I mentioned, animals have no responsibility. They do not work to improve God's creation. They have no mission other than looking out for their own physical well-being.

Today, Western society is experiencing a marriage crisis. In 1990, the marriage rate in the US was 9.8 per 1000 people. As of 2020, that number had fallen to 5.1 per 1000. Essentially, people are marrying at half the rate that they were marrying 30 years ago. And yet, despite this collapse of marriage, sexual activity among young people remains as pervasive as ever. In other words, more and more young Americans are choosing to *mate*, but not to *marry*.

When Adam and Eve gave in to their desires and ate the forbidden fruit they were ashamed. Shame is what we feel when our behavior doesn't live up to who we are supposed to be. Humans feel shame because we have a higher purpose. We are not supposed to live for the thrill of the moment without any regard for the consequences. We are responsible beings.

The marriage crisis is not only about marriage. It is a symptom of a wider crisis of responsibility. And this has everything to do with faith in God. If there is no God, then I have no mission. If I have no mission, I am not responsible. If I am not responsible, my only reason for living is my own material and physical well-being. I have become indistinguishable from the animal kingdom.

God created us "to work and to protect," to be responsible for the world He created. There is no greater expression of this mission than getting married and building a family. Through the covenant of marriage, man and woman not only fulfill their responsibilities to each other but to God Himself.

Noach
Genesis 6:9-11:32

The Flood, the Tower, and the Battle for Western Civilization

T HE PORTION OF the Bible, titled Noach, tells the stories of
two failed societies. In each of these two stories, we encounter
a breakdown in values that leads to dissolution and destruction.
First, the generation of the flood.

> *The earth was corrupt before God, and the earth was filled
> with violence. And God looked on the earth, and behold,
> it was corrupt; for all flesh had corrupted its way upon the
> earth. (Genesis 6:11-12).*

The Hebrew word translated here as "violence" is *hamas*, a
word whose precise meaning is vague. It appears to be a general
term for lawlessness and cruelty. According to the Jewish sages,
hamas refers to rampant theft, violence, rape, and general disre-
gard for law and order. The final phrase in the verses cited above,
"for all flesh had corrupted its way upon the earth," is understood

to refer to a complete breakdown of sexual boundaries between the sexes and even between animals and humans.

The second society we encounter is that of the Tower of Babel. Here, the nature of their wrongdoing is unclear from the Bible. All the Bible tells us is everyone gathered to build a tower. Why did God disperse them? The text is so vague that the Talmud was led to ask "What did they do?" (Sanhedrin 109a). The Talmud proceeds to list numerous suggestions as to what sinister motives they possessed. Most of the opinions point to some motive of rebellion against God.

I'd like to suggest that two phrases in this story reveal what was really going on. First is the opening verse of the story:

And the entire earth was one language and single ideas. (Genesis 11:1).

A few verses later, we see that it was this characteristic of "one language and single ideas" that concerned God and led to His response:

And the Lord said, "Behold, they are one people, and they all have the same language. And this is what they have started to do, and now nothing which they plan to do will be impossible for them." (Genesis 11:6).

The second phrase that reveals the true nature of this society is found in their declaration of their plans for the tower:

And they said, "Come, let's build ourselves a city, and a tower whose top will reach into heaven, and let us make a name for ourselves; otherwise we will be scattered abroad over the face of all the earth."

Why did they want to build a city and a tower? Was it to better care for the needy? Was it to use the tower in the service of God?

"Let us make a name for ourselves." The generation of the Tower of Babel sought to glorify not God, but themselves.

Let's return for a moment to the first problem with this society. Why was God so concerned that everyone had "the same language?" Why is this a problem? And why did God say that "nothing which they plan to do will be impossible for them?"

I'd like to suggest that the leaders of the Tower of Babel society were the first totalitarian dictators. Totalitarians have always needed to remove any possibility of dissent and difference of opinion as a precondition to hanging on to their power. Control of information by criminalizing dissent is critical to wielding total control over society. Alongside this control of information, such dictators also typically engage in projects designed to aggrandize themselves in the eyes of the public such that people are led to believe that they cannot survive independently of these all-powerful governing authorities. By "making a name for ourselves" and suppressing dissent, dictators throughout history have made it nearly impossible for those who live under them to disperse and seek their freedom and independence.

The generations of the flood and the Tower of Babel represent two ways that a healthy and free society can lose its way. Unfortunately, in today's Western world, we see indications that both these templates of societal decay are afoot.

Rampant crime, looting, and the breakdown of sexual boundaries are endemic problems sweeping the US and European nations alike. At the same time, we see heavy-handed censorship that demands uniformity of speech and thought, coupled with Communist-style promotion of the all-powerful state as the only path to survival. Tragically, this has become the direction of the current US government in cooperation with media and corporate elites who seek to limit personal freedom and undermine traditional Biblical values. The flood and the tower are both alive and well in our times.

In the words of Ecclesiastes,

> *What has been, it is what will be, And what has been done, it is what will be done. So there is nothing new under the sun. (Ecclesiastes. 1:9).*

The Biblical narratives of the generation of the flood and the Tower of Babel are, tragically, as relevant today as they ever were. These stories are followed by the introduction of Abraham, whom we will meet in next week's Bible portion. Then, as now, the answer to the dangers of the flood and the tower is the path of Abraham, the father of faith, who dared to call out the name of God in a hostile world.

We must continue to fight for the eternal values of law, order, personal freedom, and humility before God.

Lech Lecha

Genesis 12:1–17:27

When God Confuses Us

HAS GOD EVER thrown you a curveball? Of course, He has. There's an old Yiddish expression, "Man plans, and God laughs." We wake up every morning with an idea of what the future looks like. We make plans, as we must, only to be blindsided by God. The surprises God throws at us are sometimes blessings, sometimes, they challenge us to the core. And more often than not, we don't even know what's a blessing and what is a challenge until years later. But one thing is certain: God does not reveal His plans.

Now, you may be thinking, "What do you mean? Of course, God reveals His plans. It's called prophecy." Yes, the Bible is filled with God's word telling us what the future holds. But here's the thing: We still don't know. God still surprises us.

We might be inclined to think that we are so confused by God due to our limited understanding. Maybe we're jumping to foolish conclusions. But this is incorrect. To quote Isaiah,

"For My thoughts are not your thoughts, nor are your ways My ways," says the Lord. "For as the heavens are higher than

the earth, so are My ways higher than your ways, and My thoughts than your thoughts." (Isaiah 55:8-9).

This passage does not merely mean that God knows things He hasn't told us yet. It means that there is a fundamental human inability to understand God's thoughts and plans. And this isn't a bug in the system. It's a feature.

In fact, the inability to understand God's plans for our lives is a central theme in the life of the father of monotheistic faith, Abraham himself.

In the very first story about Abraham, we read that Abraham was sent by God to "the land that I will show you" (Genesis 12:1). But almost immediately after arriving in the land, God brought a famine that forced Abraham to leave. In one of the last stories of Abraham's life, the binding of his son Isaac, God first tells Abraham to sacrifice his son, only to later retract that command and insist that Abraham not harm Isaac at all. There are numerous examples of God sending Abraham mixed messages.

Perhaps the best example of this phenomenon is found in the birth of Ishmael.

When God first spoke to Abraham and told him to go to the promised land, He told Abraham that He would make Abraham a great nation. Despite this promise, Abraham and Sarah remained childless for many years. After Abraham's victory in a local battle to save his nephew Lot, God promised Abraham a "great reward" (Genesis 15:1). Abraham responded by pointing out that God had yet to give him children to inherit any reward God would give him. God responded by promising Abraham that he would have a child "from your own body" (Genesis 15:4).

Immediately after this prophetic promise, lo and behold, Sarah approached Abraham with the suggestion that Abraham take Sarah's maidservant Hagar to have a child with her. After all, Sarah was in her late seventies and was far past child-bearing age. It's not difficult to imagine what was going through Abraham's mind. Think about it. God promises Abraham that he will have a child from his own body. Sarah then offers Hagar as a mother for Abraham's child. There is no doubt that Abraham thought that the child born to him from Hagar was going to be the one who would inherit him and be the bearer of Abraham's covenant with God. Abraham was certain that this child, Ishmael, would be the one to become a great nation as numerous as "the stars of the heaven." (Genesis 15:5). He was certain that Ishmael's descendants would go into slavery in Egypt and be redeemed "with great wealth" (Genesis 15:13-14).

We know that Abraham thought that Ishmael was the son who would carry forward the covenant because Abraham said as much. Twelve years after the birth of Ishmael, God again spoke to Abraham. In this vision, God told Abraham that Sarah, at 90 years old, would give birth to a son who would become the bearer of the covenant. How did Abraham react?

And Abraham said to God, "Oh, that Ishmael might live before You!" (Genesis. 17:18).

In other words, Abraham did not see the necessity for the miracle of Sarah bearing a child in her old age. After all, Abraham already had a son named Ishmael. To disabuse Abraham of his misunderstanding, God immediately and emphatically responded.

Then God said: "No, Sarah, your wife shall bear you a son, and you shall call his name Isaac; I will establish My covenant with him for an everlasting covenant, and with his descendants after him." (Genesis. 17:19).

Imagine Abraham's surprise. For 12 years, he was absolutely certain that Ishmael was the son who would inherit the covenant. After all, wasn't Ishmael born as a direct result of Abraham's prayer to God asking for a child? How could there be any other way to understand what happened? But Abraham was wrong.

Abraham was the very first person to profess faith in God. And yet, even Abraham was kept in the dark as to God's plans for his life. But Abraham's faith was not shaken by this confusion. He continued to trust God and to serve Him with perfect obedience.

Too often, when people are confused about God's plan when things don't work out as expected, their faith is shaken. My friends, we must all learn a lesson from Abraham's life. God doesn't want us to know His plans; He wants us to believe in Him.

Vayeira

Genesis 18:1-22:24

The Prayer That Saved the World

I N THE PORTION of Bereishit (Genesis 18:1 - 22:24), we see how a feature of Abraham's life was his confusion about God's plan. In Bereishit, we encounter numerous examples of this phenomenon. One such episode is the narrative of Sodom and Gomorrah.

God told Abraham that he planned to destroy these wicked cities, followed by the longest sustained prayer in the Bible. Abraham pleaded and argued with God, trying to reverse the decree. When all was said and done, The answer to Abraham's prayers was a resounding "No." Sodom and Gomorrah were to be destroyed.

All this begs the question: Why did God tell Abraham that He planned to destroy these cities? God knew that no prayers from Abraham would change His mind. What was the point of telling Abraham, causing him to pray, only to ignore those prayers?

Just before God told Abraham about his decision to destroy Sodom and Gomorrah, the Bible tells us why God told Abraham his plan. While the Bible is filled with scenes of God speaking to people, it almost never tells us why God spoke to a particular person and why He decided to say what He said. And yet, here God does exactly that.

Then the Lord said, "Shall I hide from Abraham what I am about to do? Abraham will surely become a great and powerful nation, and all nations on earth will be blessed through him. For I have chosen him, so that he will direct his children and his household after him to keep the way of the Lord by doing what is right and just, so that the Lord will bring about for Abraham what he has promised him." (Genesis 18:17-19).

This passage is confusing. In justifying why God told Abraham about His plans, God reiterates Abraham's covenantal mission to transform the world, blessing all nations on earth through teaching righteousness and justice. But what does this have to do with the destruction of Sodom and Gomorrah? How does Abraham's awareness of the impending destruction serve His mission? Was God setting up Abraham, causing him to pray to save these cities, only to destroy them?

Later in the story, on the morning after the destruction, we find Abraham returning to the place where he had prayed.

Early the next morning Abraham got up and returned to the place where he had stood before the Lord. He looked down toward Sodom and Gomorrah, toward all the land of the plain, and he saw dense smoke rising from the land, like smoke from a furnace. (Genesis 19:27-28).

Here, we find Abraham faced with the reality that Sodom and Gomorrah were destroyed. Imagine what was going through his mind as he stood there surveying the destruction, watching as his prayers literally went up in smoke.

But the very next verse tells us that God did, in fact, answer Abraham's prayers, even if Abraham himself was completely unaware.

So when God destroyed the cities of the plain, he remembered Abraham, and he brought Lot out of the catastrophe that overthrew the cities where Lot had lived. (Genesis 19:29).

At first glance this seems like a minor concession to Abraham. After all, Abraham never once mentioned Lot in his prayers to save Sodom and Gomorrah. The decree to destroy the cities would not be reversed, but Lot, Abraham's nephew, would be spared. Was this the answer to Abraham's prayers?

The Bible goes on to tell us that Lot fled from the city with his family, and his wife was killed along the way, becoming a pillar of salt as she hesitated and looked back at the overturned city. Lot escaped with only his two daughters to a nearby cave. There, Lot's daughters got him drunk and had relations with him on successive nights. Both daughters became pregnant. Both gave birth to boys.

The older daughter had a son, and she named him Moab; he is the father of the Moabites of today. The younger daughter also had a son, and she named him Ben-Ammi; he is the father of the Ammonites of today. (Genesis 19:37-38).

The nations of Ammon and Moab would become enemies of Israel. How is this an answer to Abraham's prayers? How is this a sign that God "remembered Abraham" during the destruction?

Although Ammon and Moab became enemies of Israel, many generations later the nation of Moab would produce a young woman named Ruth. Ruth the Moabite would selflessly join the nation of Israel after relocating to Bethlehem with her impoverished mother in-law Naomi. Ruth eventually married Boaz and became the great-grandmother of none other than King David.

King David, of course, was the beginning of the royal Davidic line that would ultimately produce the Messiah, the savior not only of Israel, but of the entire world.

Remember God's explanation for why He told Abraham about His plans to destroy Sodom and Gomorrah?

Abraham will surely become a great and powerful nation, and all nations on earth will be blessed through him. For I have chosen him, so that he will direct his children and his household after him to keep the way of the Lord by doing what is right and just, so that the Lord will bring about for Abraham what he has promised him."

Now it all makes sense. Abraham's prayer to save Sodom and Gomorrah was motivated by his love and concern for all people. It was exactly this prayer that led to the birth of Moab, and, eventually the Messiah himself.

We have all had the experience of praying fervently for something specific only to see our prayers rejected. It can seem to us that God is not even listening. Many people have a crisis of faith when they experience their prayers being rejected. But we must always remember what the Bible tells us,

The Lord is near to all who call on him, to all who call on him in truth. He fulfills the desires of those who fear him; he hears their cry and saves them. (Psalm 145:18-19).

From Abraham's perspective, he tried to save Sodom and Gomorrah and failed. As far as he could see, the answer to his prayers was "no." But beyond Abraham's limited vision, his prayer was so powerful and so successful that it saved the entire world, even if Abraham himself had no idea.

Chayei Sarah

Genesis 23:1-25:18

Ishmael's Repentance

"Avraham expired and died in a good old age, old and satisfied, and he was gathered to his people. His sons Yitzhak and Yishmael buried him in the Machpelah cave in the field of Ephron, son of Tzohar, the Hittite, which faces Mamre." *(Genesis 25:8-9).*

RABBI SHLOMO BEN Yitzchak, known as Rashi (11th century France), the greatest and most studied of all Jewish Bible commentators, comments that the fact that Isaac, the younger son, is mentioned before Ishmael, the elder, implies that Ishmael gave precedence to Isaac as Abraham's primary son. This is viewed as evidence that Ishmael repented. Rashi goes on to explain that this is the meaning of the phrase "old and satisfied." In other words, Ishmael's repentance while Abraham was still alive brought Abraham a great measure of contentment in his old age.

The reason that Ishmael's acceptance of the primacy of Isaac is evidence of repentance is that it shows that he accepted his father's and God's decision that Isaac, rather than Ishmael himself, would be the sole heir to Abraham's blessings. Why does this acceptance by Ishmael bring such contentment to Abraham? Perhaps there is more to Ishmael's repentance.

The Midrash, a wide-ranging collection of writings from the Jewish sages, mostly from over 1000 years ago, includes traditions that expand on the stories in the Bible. The Midrashic stories provide deeper insight into the Biblical text by presenting possible background stories using the characters and storylines of the Bible as a starting point. One of the books of Midrash, called Chapters of Rabbi Eliezer, records a narrative of Ishmael's life after he was banished from the house of Abraham.

Ishmael dwelled in the wilderness of Paran (Genesis 21:21). Ishmael sent for and took a wife from the plains of Moab. Her name was Issa. Three years later, Abraham went to see his son Ishmael. He swore to Sarah that he would not get down off his camel in the place where Ishmael was encamped. He arrived there at midday and found Ishmael's wife there. He said to her, "Where is Ishmael?" She said, "He and his mother have gone to bring fruit and dates from the wilderness." He said, "Give me a bit of water and a bit of bread, for I am tired from traveling in the wilderness." She said, "There is no bread and no water." He said, "When Ishmael returns, tell him as follows. Tell him that an old man came from the land of Canaan to see you and said 'The doorstep to the house is broken.'"

When Ishmael came home his wife told him these things. He banished her. He sent his mother to bring him a wife from her father's house. Her name was Petumah. After another three years, Abraham went to see his son Ishmael. He swore to Sarah, as the first time, that he would not get off his camel in the place where Ishmael was encamped. He arrived there at midday and found Ishmael's wife there. He said to her,

"Where is Ishmael?" She said, "He went with his mother to graze the camels in the wilderness." He said, "Give me a bit of water and a bit of bread, for I am tired from traveling." She took some out and gave him. Abraham stood there and prayed to God for his son, and Ishmael's house became filled with goodness and myriad blessings. When Ishmael came home his wife told him what had happened and Ishmael knew that now his father's mercies were upon him." (PdRE, ch. 30)

We know from a number of biblical stories that hospitality and kindness were hallmarks of Abraham's values. For example, when three angels in the guise of men visited Abraham, he went beyond the call of duty in his efforts to host them (Genesis 18:1-8). Later, the "men," who were really angels, arrived in Sodom and were treated very hospitably by Abraham's nephew Lot, who grew up in Abraham's house (Genesis 19:1-3). Lot stayed true to the values Abraham and Sarah raised him with and welcomed the men despite the fact that accepting guests was frowned upon in Sodom, as we can see from the rest of the story there. (see. Gen. 19) And then, in Chayei Sarah, when Abraham sent his servant to his family to find a wife for his son Isaac, Abraham's servant devised a test to determine who is the right girl for Isaac.

May it be that when I say to a young woman, 'Please let down your jar that I may have a drink,' and she says, 'Drink, and I'll water your camels too'—let her be the one you have chosen for your servant Isaac (Genesis 24:14).

The trait that would decide who would marry Isaac was all about hospitality. When the servant then experienced the extreme hospitality of Rebekah, he knew that she was the right girl to marry Isaac(Genesis 24:17-21).

Ishmael's first wife did not reflect the values of his father's house. Apparently, Ishmael had rejected his father's teaching of hospitality. Perhaps his distance from his father's values was due to resentment stemming from his banishment. Whatever the reason, Ishmael, unlike his cousin Lot, did not continue the ways of hospitality after leaving the house of Abraham.

Later, Ishmael realized that the woman that he married was not someone whom his father approved. He realized that he had strayed from the good ways of hospitality and kindness. He searched for a second wife who would share those values. His criteria for a wife were now the same as the criteria for the wife of Isaac. She must share the value of hospitality. For Ishmael to recognize this meant that he had overcome his resentment towards and rejection of his father and all that he stood for. Although he had been banished and lived a life distant from Abraham, Ishmael realized that he still retained the values with which he was raised as a part of who he was. This realization of the goodness of the values of Abraham caused Ishmael to accept the will of his father entirely, including the primacy of Isaac.

With this interpretation of Abraham and Ishmael, the sages of the Midrash are teaching us an important lesson.

It is often that as people grow older and build their own independent lives, they forsake the teachings and values with which they were raised. This may be done out of a sense of resentment or a desire to break free. It is often many years before we accept that the teachings of our parents are within us. They shape our sense of right and wrong for life.

Parents who see their children stray from the values that they hold dear often get a sense that all is lost and that their child is no longer their child. Abraham had this same worry. From the moment that Abraham threw Ishmael out of the house, he never stopped worrying about him. After Abraham's first visit he probably went home shaking his head and wondering if all was lost, if his son forgot how he was raised. A few years later, Abraham lived to see his son's return to the values of the family.

Most parents of stray "Ishmaels" do not merit to see the return of their children. Abraham was fortunate in this regard. This is the meaning of the second statement of Rashi with which we began: "This [i.e., Ishmael's repentance] is the meaning of 'good old age' stated regarding Abraham."

Esau's Exhaustion

"Jacob was cooking a stew, Esau came from the open and he was exhausted. Esau said to Jacob, 'Feed me, please, from this red, red stuff, for I am exhausted.' He was, therefore, named Edom [red].

Jacob said, 'First, sell your birthright to me.' Esau said, 'Behold, I am going to die, and of what use is this birthright to me?' Jacob said, 'Swear to me first.' He swore to him and sold his birthright to Jacob.

Jacob gave Esau bread and a pottage of lentils. He ate, drank, got up, and left. Thus did Esau spurn the birthright" (Genesis 25:29-34).

I N THIS PASSAGE, Esau comes in from the field exhausted and sells his birthright as the firstborn to Jacob to get some pottage.

At first glance, it appears that Esau's motivation was fatigue and hunger. A common question regarding this passage is concerned with whether Jacob was taking advantage of a suffering Esau. After all, as Esau himself said, "Behold, I am going to die." The plain meaning of Esau's words is that he was so exhausted and worn out from "the field" that he was on the brink of collapse. Think of a runner who has just crossed the finish line of a marathon. Esau felt that if he didn't eat and drink immediately, he would die. He was desperate and probably not thinking clearly. Jacob thus took advantage of Esau's vulnerable state. Understood this way, the situation does not reflect well on our patriarch, Jacob.

But as we will see from a careful reading of the text, this understanding of what took place is mistaken. Let's begin with a simple question. How tired was Esau? What did he mean when he said that he was "going to die"?

The final verse of the passage quoted above states:

"He ate, drank, got up, and left. And Esau spurned the birthright."

This verse is strange for a few reasons. First, we must notice that the Bible does something unusual. Biblical narratives rarely ever include minor details along the lines of what we might call, "stage direction." It is highly unusual for the Bible to tell us that someone "got up and left" at the end of a scene. The Bible simply doesn't describe such common and insignificant actions. In light of this, we must conclude that the fact that Esau "got up and left" plays a key role in the story.

The second problem with the verse is the order of the statements. Why is the phrase "And Esau spurned the birthright" written last, after telling us, "He ate, drank, got up, and left"? To put the question another way, at what point in the scene did Esau spurn the birthright? Doesn't it make more sense to put this phrase after Esau made his derisive statement about the birthright and then sold it to Jacob?

If it is correct that Esau was so exhausted that he was literally about to die or even collapse, it is highly unlikely that after eating a warm meal, he would quickly get up and leave. The immediacy of the four verbs – "ate, drank, got up, and left" – implies that he sat down, quickly downed some hot food and some drink, and then was off again. This is not the behavior of someone who, moments ago, was about to collapse. If Esau really was as tired as the common understanding suggests, it is more likely that after a warm meal, he would have fallen asleep. By breaking with common Biblical style and telling us the seemingly trivial detail that Esau "got up and left" after eating, the Bible is telling us that his declaration "'Behold, I am going to die,'" does not mean what we thought it meant at first glance.

In light of this we may ask the following. Esau's full statement is, 'Behold, I am going to die, and of what use is this birthright to me?' What does the fact that Esau was tired and hungry at that moment have to do with the value of birthright? If Esau was in no danger, if he wasn't exhausted to the point of collapse, what could he have meant by this statement? Certainly, the birthright has value regardless of whether or not he is hungry and tired right now.

The commentator Rabbi Hezekiah ben Manoah (13th century France), known as Chizkuni, explains what Esau meant:

"'Behold, I am going to die:' The inheritance of the land of Israel is dependent on the birthright. This inheritance is not coming for another four hundred years. (See Genesis 15:13) Since I will not live until that time – i.e. 'Behold, I am going to die,' – what value is there for me in the birthright? What do I lose by selling it?"

According to Chizkuni's reading, Esau's statement that he is "going to die" was not meant as a statement of his immediate condition at that moment. Rather, Esau was saying that since he is a mortal human being with a finite life span, there is no value to him in a long-term promise from God, a promise that will only be fulfilled long after he is dead and gone. When Esau said, "of what use is this birthright to me," what he meant was simple. Because he personally would not enjoy the blessings of the birthright, Esau has no interest in it. Esau cared only about the here and now. He had no regard for his descendants, who would live long after he was gone.

If he himself cannot be a part of the blessing, then Esau wants no part of it. The promise of a great covenantal future, including centuries of suffering in exile followed by redemption; the promise and mission of being God's chosen nation through a long history, all of this meant nothing to Esau.

The birthright of the People of Israel is to be found in the future, not in the here and now.

God's blessing to the Jewish people is that in the future, the redemption of our nation and universal knowledge and acceptance of God will come about through us. The centuries of Jews who lived in the most extreme darkness of exile held fast to this birthright. Had they taken the Esau attitude of living for themselves and caring little about the distant future, we would not be here today.

The hills and valleys of the Land of Israel are filling with Jews. The footsteps of redemption have begun. Throughout our history, we have had Esaus among us who "ate, drank, got up, and left," never to be part of the Jewish People again. They and their children do not share in the unfolding blessings of redemption. It is the Jacobs of Jewish history who brought us here. They share in the redemption because we are their children. This Jacob view of the birthright of Israel is captured in the famous paraphrase of Maimonides twelfth principle of faith, printed at the end of the liturgy recited by Jews every morning.

"I believe with perfect faith in the coming of the Messiah, and even though he may delay, nevertheless, I anticipate every day that he will come."

Vayeitzei

Jacob's Vow: Opting Into God's Plan

A T THE BEGINNING of the Portion in the Bible titled Vayeit-zei, we find Jacob on the run. He left home in the wake of the events surrounding his acquisition of his father's blessings. Jacob's brother Esau vowed to kill Jacob after the death of their father, Isaac. At their mother Rebekah's behest, Jacob left home for the home of Laban, Rebekah's brother.

Traveling alone, Jacob stopped for the night and had a dream. In his dream, Jacob saw the famous vision of a ladder to heaven with angels ascending and descending on it. In the dream, God promised to protect Jacob on his journey.

There above it stood the Lord, and he said: "I am the Lord, the God of your father Abraham and the God of Isaac. I will give you and your descendants the land on which you are lying. Your descendants will be like the dust of the earth, and you will spread out to the west and to the east, to the north and to the south. All peoples on earth will be blessed through you and your offspring. I am with you and will watch over you wherever you go, and I will bring you back to this land. I will not leave you until I have done what I have promised you." (Genesis 28:13-15).

Early the next morning, when Jacob awoke, he made a vow to God.

Then Jacob made a vow, saying, "If I am taking and will give me food to eat and clothes to wear so that I return safely to my father's household, then the Lord will be my God and this stone that I have set up as a pillar will be God's house, and of all that you give me I will give you a tenth." (Genesis 28:20-22).

Why did Jacob make this vow? Why did Jacob say, "If God will be with me and will watch over me on this journey,"? Didn't we just read a few verses earlier that God promised that He would protect Jacob on this journey and that He would bring him back to the land? Why is Jacob now making a vow, as if he needs a guarantee from God that He will keep His word? It appears that Jacob is not confident in God's promise of protection. Otherwise, what's the point of the vow?

One traditional Jewish interpretation is that Jacob did not doubt whether God keeping His promise. Rather, Jacob was expressing doubt in himself. Jacob was worried that perhaps he would slip into sinfulness and would, therefore, lose the merit of the fulfillment of God's promise to him.

The problem with this answer is that God's promise to Jacob was not conditional. God did not tell Jacob that He would protect him and bring him back to the land only if he retained a certain level of righteousness. To suggest that God's promise was conditional even though no condition was stated opens the door to a theological question about all God's promises. Are God's promises conditional on good behavior even when no condition is stated? What would this mean for God's unconditional promises to Israel throughout the Bible?

On the other hand, if God's promise to Jacob was unconditional, as the text appears to say, what was the point of Jacob's vow? Was it merely Jacob's humility, thinking that maybe he could still lose a promise from God, even though God did not state any condition?

To answer this question, let's ask another question. Do we have the power to undo God's plan for the world? You're probably thinking, "Of course not!" But it's not so simple. Take, for example, the current state of the Jewish people in the land of Israel in our times. The millions of Jews ingathered from the four corners of the earth are a clear fulfillment of Biblical prophecy. Over and over, the Bible foretells a time in the future when, after a lengthy exile, the Jewish people will return to our homeland, take possession of it, and become, in the words of Deuteronomy 30, "more numerous and more prosperous" than our ancestors. These are God's promises that have come true.

Now, none of the millions of Jews in Israel are forced to remain here. Any citizen of Israel has the free will to pick up and leave. In fact, there are today many Israeli citizens who have moved to other countries. Imagine for a moment that every single Jew in the current state of Israel was to decide to pick up and move to another country. Is there anything preventing this? Can we use our free will to undo the promises of God? What would happen to the Biblical prophecies of the ingathering of the exiles?

The answer is that God would find another way to fulfill his promises. God does not stand in the way of our freedom to choose on an individual basis. If a given Jew chooses to leave the land and thereby chooses not to participate in the fulfillment of Biblical prophecy, God will not stand in that person's way. Think of God as a master chess player. He will undoubtedly win the game. But which exact moves He makes along the way will be a response to our choices. He will find a way to maneuver the situation so that His will is done despite our choices.

I'd like to suggest that this is how we ought to understand Jacob's vow, as well as the traditional rabbinic interpretation I mentioned above. When the rabbis suggested that Jacob was concerned that perhaps his own sinfulness would prevent God's promise from being fulfilled, he meant it. He was worried that he would acclimate himself to the sinful society that he was heading to. He feared that once acclimated, he would choose to remain there, worshipping the local gods, and never return to the land of his fathers.

"But what about God's promise?" you may ask. God would find a way to fulfill it with or without Jacob. Perhaps Jacob's repentant offspring would return at a later date, fulfilling God's promise to "bring you back to this land." Regardless of such hypothetical speculation, the point is that while the fulfillment of God's promises is certain, the manner of their fulfillment is impacted by the choices we make.

And therein lies the purpose of Jacob's vow. As we explained, the manner of fulfillment of God's promises is a combination of God's unerring and certain words and our choice to participate in the fulfillment. Jacob had no doubt in the certainty of God's promise. With his vow, Jacob committed himself to uphold his own end of the bargain.

The lesson is powerful. Although, as people of Biblical faith, we know that God's plan for the world will be done, we can choose to help bring that plan to fruition or to sit on the sidelines and watch someone else make it happen. The partnership between God and those who serve Him calls upon us to be active participants, aligning ourselves with God's promises and thus meriting to play a part in their fulfillment.

Vayishlach

Genesis 32:4-36:43

The Sciatic Nerve and the Eternity of Israel

IN VAYISHLACH, WE read of the famous struggle between Jacob and a "man" the night before Jacob's much-anticipated encounter with his brother Esau. The man turned out to be an angel. During the struggle, Jacob's hip joint was dislocated, causing him to emerge from the confrontation with a limp.

"A man wrestled with him until daybreak. He saw that he could not defeat him, and he struck the socket of his hip [alt. thigh]. Jacob's hip joint was dislocated as he wrestled with him...

The sun shone upon him as he passed Penuel, and he was limping on his hip. For this reason, the children of Israel must not eat the displaced sinew on the hip socket to this day because he struck Jacob's hip socket on the displaced sinew." (Genesis 32:25-26, 32-33).

This "displaced sinew" is otherwise known as the sciatic nerve. This commandment seems to commemorate the struggle between Jacob and the "man."

What if the "man" had struck Jacob on the arm or the head? Would the Bible have then stated a prohibition against eating arms or heads of animals? Why did the "man" just happen to strike Jacob at that exact spot on his body? The location of the wound is obviously significant enough that it results in a commandment relating to that specific limb of the body. Moreover, the Bible does not include other commandments that commemorate events from the lives of the patriarchs in Genesis. For example, no Biblically mandated law is commanded in the wake of the binding of Isaac or the sale of Joseph.

What is the meaning of this unusual prohibition?

The Sefer Hachinuch, a 13th-century book that discusses the meaning and basic rules for each of the 613 commandments in the Bible, discusses the prohibition against eating the sciatic nerve:

> "The root [meaning] of this commandment is to serve as a reminder to Israel that, although they will suffer many hardships in the exiles at the hands of the nations and at the hands of the children of Esau, they can be confident that they will never be lost. Rather, their offspring and name will always arise, and a redeemer will arrive and redeem them from hardship... The reason for this symbol is that the angel who fought with our forefather Jacob – which according to tradition was the ministering angel of Esau – attempted to uproot Jacob and his progeny from the world. "He saw that he could not defeat him," (v.26) and hurt him by striking his hip. So too, Esau's progeny afflicts the progeny of Jacob. At the end [of days] there will be redemption for [Jacob's progeny] from them." (Sefer Hachinuch, commandment 3)

Why did the angel strike Jacob's hip in his attempt to "uproot Jacob and his progeny,"? What was he trying to do?

The Hebrew word for "hip" used here is *yerech*. *Yerech* usually refers to a hip or thigh. Interestingly, the word *yerech* also has another meaning. Namely, it is used in many verses in the Bible as a euphemistic reference to the loins, the reproductive organ of man. Here are a few examples:

The descendants of Jacob numbered seventy in all; Joseph was already in Egypt. (Exodus 1:5).

He had seventy sons of his own, for he had many wives. – (Judges 8:30).

In these verses, offspring or descendants are referred to as *yotzei yerech,* literally, "those who emerge from the thigh." (see also Genesis 46:26).

Based on this, I would like to suggest that the angel of Esau who wrestled with Jacob was attempting to cut off Jacob's ability to reproduce, to destroy his future. In the words of the Sefer Hachinuch cited above, he "attempted to uproot Jacob and his progeny from the world."

Esau was the grandfather of the archenemy of the People of Israel, Amalek. Later, after the Exodus from Egypt, the nation of Amalek, Esau's descendants, attacked the children of Israel (Exodus 17:8). In a fascinating commentary on this episode, the Jewish sages of the Midrash homiletically described the attack as follows.

"Rabbi Hinena bar Shikla taught: 'What were the Amalekites doing [when they attacked Israel]? They were cutting off Israel's circumcisions and casting them heavenward and saying [to God] "Is this what you have chosen? Take for yourself what you have chosen!"'" (Midrash Tanhuma, Ki Tetzei:10)

It is important to note that Midrashic comments such as this are not meant to be taken literally. The ancient Jewish sages used this kind of embellishment of Biblical stories as a method of commentary. The sages would routinely "add" details to the stories in the Bible to highlight lessons they wished to derive from the narratives. Why did the sages suggest that Amalek was castrating the children of Israel when they attacked them?

Let's put these two Biblical stories together. Here in Genesis 32, the angel of Esau wrestled with Jacob. This confrontation foreshadowed the eternal struggle between Esau's offspring and Jacob's. In the course of this struggle, Esau's angel struck Jacob on the inner thigh. Centuries later, shortly after the children of Israel left Egypt in Exodus 17, Esau's descendants attacked the descendants of Jacob in almost the same spot on the body.

What does all this mean?

The special covenant of Abraham that binds Israel to God is made through circumcision. Circumcision, the removal of the foreskin, declares that even the most physical, most natural elements of a person must be consecrated to God. Circumcision says that no area of life is too natural or physical to be controlled by His will.

Rabbi Judah Leow, the great 16th-century European rabbi known as The Maharal of Prague, explained why God commanded circumcision on the eighth day. Seven days represent creation— the natural world. The eighth day represents that which is beyond the natural creation, beyond the seven days. Circumcision happens on the eighth day because the covenant with God places Israel beyond the reach of the natural order.

The circumcision represents the idea that through a relationship with God—a covenant—Israel rises above nature. Esau rules only within nature. Esau-Amalek's only hope for victory over the supernatural People of Israel is for Israel to abandon its supernatural covenant with God. Only if the circumcision is uprooted can Esau win.

The prohibition against eating the sciatic nerve serves as an eternal reminder that, although Jacob and his offspring can be maimed by Esau – although Israel may often limp through history because of oppression at Esau's hand – the future is never in doubt. Esau's angel missed the mark. Jacob's ability to reproduce, Jacob's future, was not destroyed. Jacob's offspring, the nation of Israel – through our special covenant with God – is eternal and supernatural.

Vayeishev

Genesis 37:1-40:23

How Judah Became the Leader of Israel

C HAPTER 38 OF the book of Genesis, which falls right in the middle of the portion of the Bible, Vayeishev, recounts the story of Judah and his family. The question we will deal with today is: Why is this story here?

Just to be clear, I am not asking why this story is in the Bible. Rather, the question is why this story is recorded right here, between chapters 37 and 39 of Genesis. Allow me to explain.

Chapter 37 ends with Joseph's arrival in Egypt after the sale.

The Midianites sold him in Egypt to Potiphar, an officer of Pharaoh, the captain of the guard. (Genesis 37:36).

Then, after chapter 38, the Judah story we are discussing, chapter 39 begins as follows:

Now Joseph had been brought down to Egypt, and Potiphar, an officer of Pharaoh, the captain of the guard, an Egyptian, had bought him from the Ishmaelites who had brought him down there. (Genesis 39:1).

Chapter 39 continues with the story of Joseph's time in Egypt from his arrival there and onward.

To sum up, chapter 37 ends with Joseph's arrival in Egypt. Chapter 39 picks up the story of Joseph, right where chapter 37 left off. There is no gap in time between the events in these two chapters. Chapter 39 is the immediate continuation of the conclusion of chapter 37. Chapter 38 interrupts this narrative, which leads us back to my original question: Why is this story *here*?

You might be thinking, "Well, maybe this story is here because this is when it happened?" The problem is that this is impossible. Allow me to explain.

Chapter 38 begins as follows:

At that time, Judah left his brothers and went down to stay with a man of Adullam named Hirah. There, Judah met the daughter of a Canaanite man named Shua. He married her and made love to her; (Genesis 38:1-2).

After telling us that "At that time," Judah met and married his wife, the narrative of chapter 38 then goes on to record the following series of events:

- Judah's wife becomes pregnant and gives birth to their first child, Er
- Judah's wife becomes pregnant and gives birth to their second child, Onan
- Er grows up and marries Tamar
- Er dies
- Onan then marries Tamar

- Onan dies
- Tamar is told to wait until Judah's third son, Shelah grows up and is old enough to marry her
- Judah's wife dies
- Tamar waits until Shelah grows up, but Shelah does not marry her
- Judah mistakes Tamar for a prostitute and has relations with her; Tamar becomes pregnant
- Tamar gives birth to twins, Peretz and Zerah

The Bible does not tell us exactly how long this story took to play out. We are not told the ages of the participants. That said, we can assume that, at minimum, this story lasted approximately two decades. To illustrate the point, chapter 38 begins *before* Judah meets his wife and then describes how two of Judah's sons from that wife grew up and married Tamar. What is the bare minimum for just this part of the story? How old were Er and Onan when they married Tamar? But chapter 38 doesn't end there. We then have a delay of a number of years, presumably while Judah's third son grew old enough to marry Tamar as well. This is followed by Judah's eventual union with Tamar leading to the birth of two more children.

To answer our question, we must remember Judah's role in selling Joseph. The other brothers originally wanted to kill Joseph, but Judah devised the plan to sell him instead.

Judah said to his brothers, "What will we gain if we kill our brother and cover up his blood? Come, let's sell him to the Ishmaelites and not lay our hands on him; after all, he is our brother, our own flesh and blood." His brothers agreed. (Genesis 37:26-27).

This is the first time in the Bible that we see Judah speak or take any leadership role among the sons of Jacob. While Judah's conduct here appears commendable at first glance, after all, he saved Joseph's life, the Jewish sages were critical of Judah. The rabbis explain (Bereshit Rabbah 85) that we see from Judah's words to his brothers that he knew that what they were doing was wrong. Therefore, Judah should have stopped the plot against Joseph and safely brought Joseph back to Jacob.

To put this another way, the other brothers may have justified their conduct in their own minds. They were ready to kill Joseph. But Judah's conscience bothered him. He knew what they were doing was wrong. And yet, he didn't end the plot completely. Not wanting to put himself at risk by protecting Joseph from the other brothers, he failed to take full responsibility when he saw injustice being committed.

Then we read the story of Judah and his family. We read of Judah first failing to take full responsibility for Tamar. Judah did not fulfill his commitment to her to give his third son Shelah, to her as a husband. We then see Judah slip into immoral behavior, thinking Tamar was a prostitute. But then the story takes a critical turn.

When Judah thought Tamar was a prostitute, Judah gave her his cord and staff as collateral until he could send proper payment. After it was discovered that Tamar was pregnant, Judah, not knowing that he was the father, ordered Tamar be brought out to be put to death for her immorality.

As she was being brought out, she sent a message to her father-in-law. "I am pregnant by the man who owns these," she said. And she added, "See if you recognize whose seal and cord and staff these are." Judah recognized them and said, "She is more righteous than I, since I wouldn't give her to my son Shelah." And he did not sleep with her again. (Genesis 38:25-26).

Notice that Tamar did not say, "Judah is the father." She merely presented the cord and staff and asked Judah to identify the owner. Had Judah decided to protect himself from shame, he could have easily denied ownership of the items. But this time Judah took responsibility. He admitted guilt and humbled himself, recognizing not only that he was wrong to sentence Tamar to death but that he was wrong in withholding Shelah as well, not to mention the embarrassment he incurred by being exposed to all as having solicited the services of what he thought was a prostitute.

After this story, throughout the rest of the book of Genesis, it is Judah who is the unequivocal leader of the sons of Jacob. It is Judah who takes responsibility and at risk to his own life, to save Benjamin. And it is Judah who is eventually blessed with the eternal kingship of Israel.

I'd like to suggest that the words "At that time" at the beginning of Genesis 38 refer to the end of the story. In other words, in the wake of Joseph's sale, Judah decided that he would never again shirk responsibility, even if it meant risking his own life and honor. Then, when confronted by his own guilt in the Tamar situation, Judah publicly repented and took full responsibility, regardless of the damage to his reputation. Genesis 38 interrupts the Joseph story because Judah's personal development was a direct result of Judah's own feelings of guilt in the wake of the sale of his brother.

Genesis 38 is the story of Judah's emergence as Israel's leader and forefather of the royal line of David. The Bible teaches that the prerequisites of this leadership are humility, admission of one's own guilt before God and man, and doing what is right regardless of the risk to one's own status and even one's own life.

Miketz
Genesis 41:1-44:17

The Spirit of God in Joseph

THE PORTION OF Miketz opens up with a description Paroah's dreams After Pharaoh's wizards and wise men fail to interpret the dreams accurately, Joseph is summoned from prison. His interpretations rang true to Pharaoh. Pharaoh was impressed. What impressed Pharaoh was not only that he interpreted the dreams, but what Joseph added to the interpretation. Joseph described the seven years of plenty followed by seven years of famine that are foretold in the dreams, but he did not stop there. Joseph proceeded to present a comprehensive economic plan to prevent the seven years of famine from hurting Egypt. At this point Pharaoh expressed his admiration for Joseph.

> *"Pharaoh said to his servants, 'Can one such as this be found, a man in whom is the spirit of God?'" (Genesis 41:38).*

The Hebrew word for "spirit of God" is ru'ach Elohim. What precise characteristics are implied by this term? It is clear that Pharaoh was impressed with Joseph. Obviously, Pharaoh was not speaking in Biblical Hebrew but in the ancient Egyptian tongue.

In other words, the Bible here is translating what Pharaoh said into Hebrew. What did Pharaoh mean when he referred to Joseph as being filled with *ru'ach Elohim*?

The term "spirit of God"—ru'ach Elo-him—appears in two other contexts in the Bible. The first is in the second verse, right at the beginning.

> *In the beginning, G-d created the heavens and the earth. The earth was unformed and empty, and darkness covered the surface of the abyss, and the spirit of God – ru'ach Elo-him – hovered above the surface of the water. (Genesis 1:1-2).*

The third mention of this term appeared when Betzalel was introduced in the book of Exodus. God chose Betzalel to be the chief craftsman and architect of the Tabernacle, the portable temple built in the desert.

> *God spoke to Moses, saying, "See, I have called by name [i.e. designated] Betzalel, son of Uri, son of Chur, of the tribe of Yehudah. I have filled him with the spirit of God – ru'ach Elo-him – with wisdom, understanding, knowledge, and [skill to perform] all types of crafting." (Exodus 31:1-3).*

In this case, the Bible elaborates on the meaning of the term ruach Elo-him, adding that it embodies wisdom, understanding, knowledge, and practical skill.

God endowed Betzalel with the ability to build and craft the Tabernacle and everything in it. God's instructions to Moshe were relayed to Betzalel, who was then responsible for the actual fashioning of these objects.

The connection between these two uses of the term *ru'ach*

Elo-him in Exodus and at the beginning of the creation story is quite clear. Immediately after the first two verses of the creation story, the Bible relates the very first event of creation.

God said, "Let there be light." (Gen. 1:3)

The name for God used here—o—is the name associated with G-d as creator. Only this name is used throughout the creation story in Genesis 1. This characteristic of God—ru'ach Elo-him— implies God's creative power.

Betzalel's job also involved creation. He was to actualize God's will by building specific objects. The Jewish sages of the Talmud saw a connection between the creation story in Genesis and Betzalel's role in building the Tabernacle.

Betzalel knew how to combine the letters [of the Alef – Bet] through which heaven and earth were created. – Babylonian Talmud, Berachot 55a

The sages taught us that Betzalel's construction of the Tabernacle was inspired by the same divine creativity exhibited by God in the creation story in Genesis.

Allow me to explain.

The objects in the Tabernacle were physical objects that represented abstract spiritual ideas. Betzalel knew how to take lofty spiritual ideas and actualize them in the physical world in a practical way.

The creation of heaven and earth was no different. The entire creation story is the practical physical manifestation of extremely lofty spiritual ideas. In order to create, God had to bridge the gap between abstract spirituality and physical reality. Both the creation of heaven and earth and the building of the Tabernacle represent this same idea – spiritual ideas represented in practical physical reality. This is the meaning of the statement of the sages of the Talmud.

And this is the trait that Joseph exhibited when he interpreted Pharaoh's dreams. Not only did Joseph have the ability to interpret the messages in abstract dream-state images correctly, he was also able to compose a practical plan of action to be implemented in response to these messages. He exhibited *ru'ach Elohim* – the ability to bridge the gap between the abstract spiritual and the practical physical. This understanding can help explain the following cryptic statement of the Jewish sages:

> *"And the spirit of God – ruach Elohim – hovered" (Gen 1:1) –*
> *this refers to the spirit of the Messiah." (Bereshit Rabbah 2:4).*

If *ruach Elohim* is expressed in the actualization of spiritual ideas in the physical world, there can be no greater expression of this power than the Messiah. The Messianic age is a time when the abstract spiritual potential of all of creation will be manifest in the most basic and perceptible physical reality. There will be no gap between the spiritual and the physical when the Messiah comes. Physical reality will be clearly seen as the application of God's will here on Earth.

> *"For the earth shall be filled with knowledge of G-d as waters cover the sea." (Isaiah 11:9).*

Vayigash
Genesis 44:18-47:27

Seeking the Comfort of
Exile

V AYIGASH TELLS THE story of Jacob and his sons moving to
Egypt to escape the famine in the Land of Canaan. The
great 13th-century scholar and leader Rabbi Moses ben Nach-
man, known as Nahmanides, used this scene in his commentary
on the Bible as a foreshadowing symbol of the Jewish people's
future exile.

The descent of Jacob to Egypt foreshadows our present exile…
For the sons of Jacob themselves caused their descent [to Egypt]
by selling Joseph their brother. Jacob went down there because
of the famine, thinking he would be saved with his son in the
house of one who favored them, for Pharaoh loved Joseph as his
own son. They intended to return from there with the conclusion
of the famine in Canaan as they said, 'We have come to dwell as
strangers in the land as there is no grazing for your servants' flock
since the famine is severe in the land of Canaan' (Genesis 47:4).

But behold, they did not return, and [Jacob's] exile was prolonged.
He died there, they brought up his bones [to Canaan], and the elders and officers of Pharaoh brought him up and mourned greatly.

So, too, are we with Rome and Edom [our sages' code name for the present exile]. Our brothers brought about our falling into their hands by establishing a pact and treaty with the Romans. Agrippas, the last king of the second Temple period, ran to them for assistance. Because of famine the people of Jerusalem were captured, and the exile has been very long [since then]. We do not know its end as we did with other exiles. We are as dead people in it." (*Ramban al HaTorah*, Gen. 47:28).

As Nachmanides describes here, the exile in Egypt should never have gone on as long as it did. Originally, Jacob, his sons, and their families went there as strangers in need of a temporary refuge to wait out the famine. After the famine, they stayed in Egypt. The feeling of strangeness was gone. They felt at home in Egypt.

Nachmanides explains that the beginning of exile is seeking refuge in the hands of foreign nations that love us. Pharaoh loved Joseph. He welcomed Jacob as an honored nobleman in his midst. Undoubtedly, the Egyptians' welcoming attitude to Jacob and his sons led to their feelings of comfort living there. This, Nachmanides teaches, prolongs the exile. Had they stuck to their original intentions and returned to their land when the famine had ended, there would have been no Egyptian exile.

Our Bible's portion's closing line emphasizes this point.

"Israel dwelt in the land of Egypt, in the land of Goshen. They acquired it and they were fruitful and multiplied greatly." *(Genesis 47:27).*

Targum Yonatan ben Uziel – a 2nd Temple era Aramaic translation and commentary, translates "they acquired it" as "they acquired acquisitions of land."

Rabbi Ephraim Lunshintz, (16th-17th century Europe), in his commentary on the Bible, expands on this point.

This entire verse speaks of the guilt of the Children of Israel. God decreed upon them 'that your offspring shall be strangers', and they sought to become permanent citizens in a place where they were supposed to be foreigners… This verse finds them guilty of seeking land holdings in a land that is not for them. Did they not say to Pharaoh 'We have come to dwell as strangers in the land,'? At first, they came only on a temporary basis as short-term dwellers. And now they had retracted their words. They became so permanent there that they did not want to leave until God took them out with a mighty Hand. Those who did not want to leave died in the darkness."

During the centuries of exile, no one would have imagined that Jews who would be given the opportunity and ability to return to the Land of Israel would choose not to. And yet, we see this phenomenon happening in our times. The fact that there are many American Jews with the financial resources to do so have not flocked to the modern State of Israel is emerging as one of the great failures of Jewish history. Like the early generations of Israel in Egypt, Jews in the current exile have grown quite comfortable. Too many have forgotten that exile is an undesirable predicament, that it is a punishment, that we wait in the temporary exile for the opportunity to go home.

The famine in the land is over. It's time to go home.

Vayechi

Jacob or Israel?

And Jacob lived in the land of Egypt for seventeen years. So the length of Jacob's life was one hundred and forty-seven years. When Israel's days drew close to death, he called his son Joseph and said to him, "Now if I have found favor in your sight, please put your hand under my thigh, and deal kindly and truly with me. Please do not bury me in Egypt (Genesis 47:28:29).

IN THE OPENING verses of the portion Vayechi, we find Jacob on his deathbed. Curiously, in these two consecutive verses, we see the two names of Jacob, Jacob and Israel, used seemingly interchangeably. In fact, ever since Jacob wrestled with the angel and received his new name, Israel, both names have been used by the Bible.

Contrast this with Jacob's grandfather, who, once his name was changed from Abram to Abraham, was never again referred to as Abram. Why does Jacob retain both names? This question is strengthened when we consider God's words to Jacob in Genesis 35.

And God said to him, "Your name is Jacob; your name shall not be called Jacob anymore, but Israel shall be your name." So He called his name Israel. (Genesis 35:10).

God stated clearly that Jacob "shall not be called Jacob anymore," and immediately thereafter we read:

So Jacob set up a pillar in the place where He talked with him, a pillar of stone; and he poured a drink offering on it, and he poured oil on it. And Jacob called the name of the place where God spoke with him, Bethel (Genesis 35:14-15).

To sum up our questions: Why does the Bible continue to call Jacob by his original name after God declared that he should no longer be called Jacob? In light of this, what did God mean when He said "your name shall not be called Jacob anymore, but Israel shall be your name"? Why does the Bible call him Jacob in certain situations and Israel in others?

When we look at their origins, we see that the two names, Jacob and Israel, have somewhat opposing connotations. Jacob was given his name because he followed Esau out of the womb, grasping his heel. Jacob in Hebrew, *Yaakov*, literally means "will follow." The Hebrew word for "heel" is *akev*, the same as the root of the name Yaakov. This name implies a subservient or secondary status. Israel, or *Yisrael*, on the other hand, from the root for "minister" or "overcoming" implies prominence and leadership.

We should note that both names, Jacob and Israel, are used in the Bible to refer to the entire nation of Israel. While a full treatment of the uses of these two names throughout the Bible is beyond the scope of this article, consider the following passage from Isaiah.

In that day the remnant of Israel, the survivors of Jacob, will no longer rely on him who struck them down but will truly rely on the Lord, the Holy One of Israel. A remnant will return, a remnant of Jacob will return to the Mighty God. Though your people be like the sand by the sea, Israel, only a remnant will return. Destruction has been decreed, overwhelming, and righteous. (Isaiah 10:2-22).

From this passage and numerous others, it seems that the name "Jacob" is used to describe the Jewish people when subservient to others in exile. In addition, the term "house of Jacob" which appears as a name for the nation of Israel many times in the Bible (e.g, Exodus 19:3, Psalm 114:1), seems to imply the private life of the Jewish people, closing themselves off from outside influence. This is consistent with the first description of Jacob as a "dweller of tents" (Genesis 25:27).

To sum up, when the nation of Israel retreats from leadership and influencing the world, either due to persecution and exile or the choice to insulate itself from harmful outside influences, it is called Jacob. But when Israel rises to prominence and asserts itself as a nation on the world stage, it is called Israel.

Jacob retained both his names because he continued to live in both roles. And so have the Jewish people. The Jewish people have spent much of our history as "Jacob" subservient, in exile, continually defending ourselves from outside influences that could compromise our unique identity. At the same time, we are also Israel, charged with the leadership mission to be "a kingdom of priests and a holy nation" that brings knowledge of God to all humanity.

Perhaps we can now understand the use of these two names in the opening verses of our Bible portion:

And Jacob lived in the land of Egypt for seventeen years. So the length of Jacob's life was one hundred and forty-seven years. When Israel's days drew close to death, he called his son Joseph and said to him, "Now if I have found favor in your sight, please put your hand under my thigh, and deal kindly and truly with me. Please do not bury me in Egypt. (Genesis 47:28:29).

Jacob, living in exile in the land of Egypt, wants to ensure that he will be buried in his homeland, the land promised to Abraham and Isaac. By using the name *Israel* here, the Bible is telling us that Jacob's motives were not merely about his own preference for where he would be buried. Jacob wanted to ensure that his family understood that their place was not here in Egypt, in exile, as Jacob. He wanted to make it clear to them that they must never forget that their homeland is the land that God gave them through the covenant passed down from Abraham. It was not "Jacob," the individual Jew in exile, who asked to be buried in the land of his forefathers. He made this request as "Israel."

The identification of Jews with the land of Israel as our homeland is an essential component of our national identity. It is only by living as an independent nation in the land that God gave us that we achieve the status of *Israel*, the nation that is meant to bring the light of God to the world. The desire of Jacob to be buried in the land did not come from a private, personal place. Rather, he was reminding his children, and all of us, that our true purpose is to be Israel, the ministers of God, triumphant and powerful in our land so that we can fulfill the mission of building God's kingdom on Earth.

Exodus

Shemot

Exodus 1:1 - 6:1

The Three Signs: Pharaoh's Perspective

W HEN GOD CALLED on Moses to go to Egypt and liberate the Children of Israel, Moses worried that they wouldn't believe it was God who had sent him. To help convince them, God provided Moses with three miraculous signs (Exodus 4:1-9).

The three signs were:

Moses would throw his staff on the ground. The staff would turn into a snake. When Moses grasped the tail of the snake, it would then turn back into a staff.

Moses would put his hand into his bosom. His hand would thus become "leprous like snow." When he would then put his hand back into his bosom, his hand would return to normal.

Moses would take water from the Nile and pour it on the ground. The water would turn to blood on the ground.

What is the meaning of these three signs? The commentaries offer numerous explanations, all of which explain their symbolism either to the Children of Israel or to Moses himself.

But a few verses later, God told Moses to perform these same three signs before Pharaoh.

The Lord said to Moses, "When you return to Egypt, see that you perform before Pharaoh all the wonders I have given you the power to do. But I will harden his heart so that he will not let the people go. (Exodus 4:21).

As mentioned above, the classic explanations of these signs deal with their meaning either for Moses himself or for the People of Israel. If these very same signs were also to be performed before Pharaoh, what did they mean to Pharaoh and the Egyptians? If they had no specific meaning or message for Pharaoh, God should have given Moses alternative signs to perform before Pharaoh. Surely, God has no shortage of signs!

An additional question about these three signs relates to their "rehearsal" at the burning bush. In the passage in Exodus 4, when God gave Moses the signs, He told Moses to demonstrate the first two signs right then and there, which Moses did. But He did not tell Moses to demonstrate the third sign, turning water into blood. Why did God make Moses practice the first two signs but not the third?

To understand the significance of these three signs for Pharaoh and his Egyptian advisers, we should consider what they might have meant in the context of Egyptian culture and beliefs at that time. The message of the signs would only be impactful if Pharaoh could easily comprehend it.

The first sign was turning Moses'—or Aaron's—staff into a snake and then back into a staff. Snakes symbolized magic and protection in Egypt. More specifically to Moses' sign, it was common for Egyptian gods to be depicted holding snake-wands. For example, a statuette found by archaeologists in the Ramasseum in Egypt depicts a female sau, a type of sorceress who could provide magical protection. This statuette holds a snake wand in each hand.

Perhaps Aaron's staff turning into a snake served to mock the powers of Egyptian sorcery. This point is emphasized when Aaron's staff devoured the staff-snakes of the magicians of Egypt (Exodus 7:12). By performing this sign before Pharaoh, Moses was in effect saying, "I do not believe in your gods and yet, not only is my staff a snake and vice versa, but my staff-snake can even devour yours. What of your protective and magical powers now?" With this sign, Moses and Aaron demonstrated that the power of God was greater than the power of Egyptian sorcery.

According to Sir James Frazer, author of the classic on ancient pagan religion *The Golden Bough*, Egyptians believed that leprosy afflicted sinners, in particular those who sinned by eating the flesh of a sacred animal (*Golden Bough* Ch. 49 section 4). Amazingly, it is precisely this 'sin' that Moses told Pharaoh the Israelites were going to commit by bringing animal offerings to God in the desert, as Moses made clear after the third plague:

Pharaoh summoned Moses and Aaron and said, 'Go! Bring offerings to your God in the land.' Moses said, 'It is not proper to do so, for we will offer the deity of Egypt to Hashem our God. Behold, if we were to slaughter the deity of Egypt in their sight, will they not stone us?' (Exodus 8:21-22).

Seen this way, the second sign, like the first, was a mockery of Ancient Egyptian beliefs. Moses again said, "It is our God, and not the offended Egyptian deities, who determines who does and does not have leprosy. Who is and who is not considered a sinner is in the hands of the God of Israel alone."

It is common knowledge that the Egyptians worshiped the Nile as a god. The Nile was seen as the giver and sustainer of all life. This was a natural pagan result of Egypt's dependence on the rising tides of the Nile for economic well-being.

Moses's third sign – turning water into blood – was not about just any water. God specifically told Moses to "take some water *from the river*" (4:9) and turn it into blood. "The river" obviously refers to the Nile. This explains why God did not tell Moses to rehearse the sign while standing at the burning bush – somewhere in the Sinai peninsula. The point of the sign was not to turn *water* into blood, but to turn the *Nile* into blood.

Like the first two signs, the third is a direct affront to Pharaoh's Egyptian pagan beliefs especially since the Egyptians saw Pharaoh himself as the human embodiment of the creator and protector of the Nile.

Several verses in the Bible clearly show that the primary purpose of the Ten Plagues was not the salvation of the People of Israel from Egypt. That could have been accomplished without all of the plagues. The purpose of the plagues was to refute the gods of Egypt in the eyes of the Egyptians.

"I shall harden Pharaoh's heart and I shall multiply My signs and My wonders in the land of Egypt. Pharaoh will not heed you, and I shall put My hand upon Egypt. And Egypt shall know that I am God, when I stretch out My hand over Egypt." (Exodus 7:3-5)

As we now understand, the repudiation of the gods of Egypt – the "signs" and "wonders" in this verse – began with the three signs given to Moses at the burning bush.

Va'eira
Exodus 6:2-9:35

What Does God's Name Actually Mean?

God spoke to Moses, and He said to him: I am the Lord (YHVH). I appeared to Abraham, to Isaac, and to Jacob as God Almighty (El Shaddai), but with My name "the Lord," (YHVH) I did not make myself known to them. Exodus 4:2-3).

THE OPENING VERSES of the portion called Va'eira calls our attention to God's names. Let's sum up the points that God made to Moses here:

I am YHVH
I appeared to the patriarchs as El Shaddai
I did not reveal myself to them as YHVH.

This passage is difficult to understand. After all, throughout the book of Genesis, God uses the name YHVH in His interactions with the patriarchs. So, what did God mean by this cryptic statement to Moses?

To answer this question, we must first understand the true

meaning of the Hebrew name YHVH – almost universally translated as "the Lord."

What does YHVH actually mean?

God's name, YHVH, also known as the tetragrammaton, appears over 6000 times in the Bible. Throughout most English translations of the Bible this name is translated as "the Lord." But, in fact, "the Lord" is not a translation of the tetragrammaton at all as YHVH has no meaning in Hebrew outside of being God's name.

So what does YHVH actually mean?

Like every name of God, the name YHVH is a Hebrew word. It is a very holy and lofty Hebrew word, but it is a word, nonetheless. Like every Hebrew word, YHVH has a root. The root of YHVH is the verb *to be* or *to exist*. The form or conjugation of this root, that is the name YHVH, is an impossible mix of past, present, and future tenses. We can see where God's name YHVH comes from if we consider three words:

#1 YEHYEH   Will be
#2 HOVEH   Is / Present
#3 HAYAH   Was

I will try to keep this simple. Look at these words. They have some features in common. They have some differences. Each one has an exception that the other two do not have.

#1 begins with YE	#2 & #3 begin with H
#2 contains OV in the middle	#1 & #3 do not
#3 ends with AH	#1 & #2 end with EH

Look at those three exceptions together. Look familiar? YE OV AH Let's put it all together. The name of God YHVH is made up of three syllables.

The first syllable	YE is the unique beginning of YEHYEH	"will be"
The middle syllable	OV is the unique middle of HOVEH	"present"
The last syllable	AH is the unique end of HAYAH	"was"

So, YHVH, as a Hebrew word, is a blend of the words for *future, present,* and *past.* Pretty good name for God, right?

Different parts of the four letters of YHVH contain grammatical elements of these three different tenses. The Y at the beginning indicates future tense. The oV in the middle indicates present. The aH sound at the end is for the past tense. *Future, present, past.* Does this seem out of order? Wouldn't it make more sense if the order was *past, present,* and *future*?

Everything in existence first exists in the *future.* Then it becomes part of the *present.* It then slips into the *past.* Before I sat down to write this, my writing was a part of the future. Right now, as I am writing it is in the present. After I am done, it will be part of the past. The same is true for every created being and every moment in time. So, in terms of how reality comes into being, *future, present, past* is the order of existence.

In fact, if you look back at the name YHVH as I just explained it you will see something amazing. A person reading this name would begin by starting the word for "will be". He would then continue in the next syllable by saying the word "present". He would finish the word by saying the final syllable of the word "was." His expression of God's name begins in the future, passes through the present, and ends up in the past!

We need to understand one more detail to know what this

lofty name of God means. While the word for "will be" is YE-HYEH, as we stated above, the pronunciation of the "E" in the first syllable of this word is "ee" as in "sleep" or "feet." But in God's name, the "E" in the first syllable is pronounced as "eh," like "wet" or "bed." In Hebrew these two sounds are different vowels. So what's the difference?

Without getting too complicated—unless I already have—we'll note that this difference in vowel at the beginning of a verb conjugation implies a causative tense. In other words, the true meaning of God YHVH is, "Cause of all existence in the future, present, and past." Pretty good name for God, right?

This name does not actually translate to "the Lord," which is how it is almost universally translated in all Bibles. So, if it doesn't mean "the Lord," why is it translated that way?

You see, Jewish law and tradition prohibit the explicit utterance of this holy name as it is written. This should make sense now. After all, the meaning of the name is a concept that human beings can not hold in their consciousness. *Past, present,* and *future* all blended together - as they are in God - may be something that we believe as a matter of faith, but the human experience within time prevents us from fully grasping this concept. Therefore, in deference to the fact that this name describes God in a way that is beyond our comprehension, we are prohibited from saying this name. After all, expressing something I do not know or understand is tantamount to falsehood. If I express something, I am giving the impression that it is something that I know. And this name of God is unknowable.

As I explained, thousands of years ago, we came up with a euphemism that is the standard replacement when we see the name YHVH. That euphemism is ADONAI. The translation into English of ADONAI is "my Lord," which popularly became "The Lord."

Let's now return to our original question. What did God mean when He said that he did not make Himself known to the patriarchs in Genesis as YHVH?

As we explained, YHVH describes God as the cause of all existence. Because He *is* the cause of all existence, He is the Master of all existence. While the patriarchs, Abraham, Isaac, and Jacob knew this to be true, they never experienced this side of God. More to the point, God never *revealed* Himself as Master of all existence in his dealings with the patriarchs. His mastery of existence was not on public display. Allow me to explain.

The name El Shaddai refers to God's trait of providing whatever is needed for His creations. And as we explained, God certainly looked after the needs of the patriarchs. We see Him making and fulfilling promises to them, like the promise to Abraham that Sarah would bear a child. We even see God protecting and guiding the success of the patriarchs, as He protected Jacob in the house of Laban and Joseph on his journey to Egypt.

But we don't see any overt public displays of God's mastery over creation in Genesis. There are no public miracles in the book of Genesis.

In the words of our verses here in Exodus 4,

I appeared to Abraham, to Isaac, and to Jacob as God Almighty (El Shaddai), but with My name "the Lord," (YHVH) I did not make myself known to them.

God goes on to tell Moses that this is about to change. From here on, God will perform great public acts of dominance over the created order, the Ten Plagues, the splitting of the Red Sea, and more miracles that will clearly demonstrate to all that He is YHVH, the Cause and Master over all creation.

Bo
Exodus 10:1-13:16

Torah, the Jews, and the Moon

"God said to Moses and Aaron in the land of Egypt saying: "This month shall be for you the beginning of the months – it is the first of the months of the year for you."' (Exodus 12:1-2).

THE OPENING VERSES of Exodus 12 introduce God's instructions to the children of Israel regarding the preparations for the Passover lamb leading up to the Exodus. God begins his words to Moses by telling him that the month in which the Exodus falls shall forever be known as the first month.

The "First Month" is not the beginning of the year

This does not mean the counting of years would begin that same month. Rather, the numbering of months begins with the month of the Exodus. To illustrate, when we read later on in the Bible, such verses as, "In the seventh month on the first day of the month, there shall be a day of rest for you" (Leviticus 23:24), the "seventh" month refers to the seventh month counting from the month of the Exodus, known today as the month of Nisan.

We should bear in mind that this counting of the months beginning with the month of the Exodus does not imply anything about counting years from creation. As is well known, Rosh Hashana, the Jewish new year, takes place in Tishrei, half a year removed from the month of the Exodus. It may seem strange to people used to months and years being counted together, but the New Year begins on the first day of the seventh month. Again, this is because the numbering of the months relates to the Exodus, not creation.

The 'Lunar-Solar' calendar

The great Jewish commentator Rabbi Avraham Ibn Ezra (12th cent. Spain) points out that there is no such thing as a lunar year, just as there is no such thing as a solar month. Ibn Ezra explains that the moon's cycle is slightly more than twenty-nine days long. The solar cycle is three hundred and sixty-five and one-quarter days long. Therefore, the concept of a "lunar year" is just twelve lunar cycles. The natural cycles of the moon do not have a "year." Nothing significant happens to the moon every twelve months. Similarly, the twelve "months" of the three hundred and sixty-five day solar year has nothing to do with the sun's natural cycle. The months of the solar year we are familiar with, January, February, etc., do not reflect any natural phenomenon.

To sum up, for those who may need clarification. A "month" is a lunar cycle, the entire cycle of the waxing and waning of the moon. This cycle takes 29 and a half days. There is no "year" for the moon. A "year" is a solar cycle, the time it takes for the earth to travel around the sun. There are no "months" in this cycle. Nothing happens every 30 days or so in the solar cycle.

We are used to speaking of the Jewish calendar as a lunar calendar. This is only partially accurate. As we explained, a purely lunar calendar would not have years. Rather, the Jewish / Biblical calendar is a lunar-solar calendar. We follow the lunar cycle to determine the beginning and end of each month. At the same time, we mark the years by counting twelve lunar cycles. This is the number of lunar cycles that comes closest to equaling the length of the year – i.e., one solar cycle.

Twelve lunar cycles equals 354 days. One solar year is 365 days. Due to this 11-day discrepancy, if left alone, the dates on a Hebrew calendar would be eleven days earlier each and every year. So, this calendar can create a problem. The instructions for the festivals include the season of the year that they must fall within. For example,

You shall observe the Festival of Unleavened Bread; seven days you shall eat unleavened bread, as I commanded you, at the appointed time in the month of the ripening ('Aviv in Hebrew), for during it you came out of Egypt; they shall not appear before Me empty-handed.(Exodus 23:15).

Aviv is the springtime, the time when the early grain begins to be ready for harvest. If the date of Passover was celebrated 11 days earlier in the solar cycle each year, it would not take too long for Passover to fall out in winter, then the fall, etc. To remedy Jewish law, we are required to insert an additional month every few years. This extra month readjusts the calendar so that the months will always remain in the correct seasons. To put it another way, most Jewish years have 12 months. Some Jewish years have 13 months.

The symbolism of the moon

Counting months by the moon's cycles has great spiritual significance in Judaism. Once a month, during the first half of the month – while the moon is in its growth phase – Jews will go outside at night and recite a blessing over the New Moon.

I'd like to draw attention to a few sentences of the liturgy that we recite at that time.

"May it be your will, Lord, to fill the moon so that there be no flaw in it. May the light of the moon be like the light of the sun and like the light of the seven days of creation as it was before it was diminished, as it is said: 'The two great luminaries.' (Genesis 1:16) And may we fulfill the verse that states: 'They shall seek the Lord their God, and David, their king.' (Hosea 3:5) Amen."

We pray to God that this month, He should allow the moon to continue to grow past its size when it is full until it is the size of the sun. A moon the size of the sun would have no diminution in it. This is a strange request. What does it really mean?

The moon gives off no light of its own. The light of the moon is sunlight that is reflected to Earth. But the moon reflects only a very small percentage of the sun's light. When we only see a small sliver of the moon, only a small amount of sunlight is being reflected down to us. The larger the moon, the more sunlight is reflected to Earth. When we pray for the moon's light to be identical to that of the sun, we are saying that we want the moon to somehow reflect one hundred percent of the sun's light. Only this way could the moon's light be equivalent to the sun's light.

The sun is the **source** of the light. The moon is the **reflector** of that light. God is the source of light. We, as servants of God, are supposed to act like the moon. As Jews, we see the moon as a metaphor for our mission. God is the light of good, morality, and truth. We strive to illuminate the world with God's light reflected through us to the world. Every time the moon renews itself, we see this as symbolic of another opportunity to increase the light of God in a world that is all too dark.

We pray that the amount of Godliness we reflect grows until it fills the world like the light of the sun in broad daylight. It is our fervent hope, prayer, and dream that we will somehow be able to reflect God's light so completely that the world will come to a complete and pure understanding of God.

Beshalach

Exodus 13:17-17:16

The Baal-Zephon Plan: Egypt's Final Lesson

THE BIBLE PORTION, Beshalach opens with a description of the Exodus from Egypt. After the Children of Israel journeyed for a few days, God commanded Moses to tell them to backtrack slightly and camp in a very specific location for a very specific purpose.

> *Speak to the Children of Israel and let them turn back and encamp before Pi-Hahiroth, between Migdol and the sea, before Baal-zephon; you shall encamp opposite it by the sea. Pharaoh will say of the Children of Israel, 'They are imprisoned [heb. nevuchim] in the land, the desert has locked them in.' I shall strengthen the heart of Pharaoh and he will pursue them, and I will be glorified through Pharaoh and his entire army, and Egypt will know that I am God. (Exodus 14:2-4).*

It is interesting that at the end of this passage, God told Moses that as a result of this plan, Egypt would finally know that He is God. Apparently, the Ten Plagues, including the final death of the firstborn, had failed to convince the Egyptians of the supremacy of the God of Israel.

What are the details of this plan? Let's sum up the content of these verses.

- First, the Children of Israel are to travel back toward Egypt and camp opposite Baal-zephon.
- Upon hearing about this, Pharaoh will conclude that they are "imprisoned" – or *nevuchim* – in the land and "locked in" by the desert.
- Emboldened by this conclusion, Pharaoh and his army will pursue the Children of Israel and fall right into the trap that God has set for them.
- They will then learn, once and for all, that the Lord is God.

Why there? What is the purpose of the plan?

The location where God wants Israel to camp is very specific. The Bible generally gives us detailed descriptions of locations. Yet here, we have very precise coordinates.

before Pi-Hahiroth, between Migdol and the sea, before Baal-zephon; you shall encamp opposite it by the sea.

Once the specific location at which Israel is to encamp – before Pi-Hahiroth, between Migdol and the sea – is stated, the additional detail "before Baal-zephon" seems superfluous. Haven't the directions been stated clearly enough? What is the importance of Baal-zephon.

According to the plan, it seems that Israel's encampment at Baal-zephon, specifically, will cause Pharaoh to conclude that Israel is doomed. What is it about Baal-zephon that leads Pharaoh to believe that the God who decimated Egypt with the ten plagues will not be able to save Israel from being "imprisoned" and "locked in"?

When God told Moses how Pharaoh will react to the news, He suggested that Pharaoh will say:

"They are imprisoned [nevuchim] in the land and locked in by the desert."

What exactly do these phrases mean? "Imprisoned in the land"? "Locked in by the desert"? Why not simply say that Israel is "lost" or "stranded"? Why does God suggest that this is what Pharaoh will say? Furthermore, is there a connection between these unusual phrases and Baal-zephon?

Finally, God said that at the end of this plan, the Egyptians will finally "know that I am God." The question is obvious. If the Ten Plagues, and especially the plague of the firstborn, didn't teach the Egyptians to believe in God, why do we suppose that this plan will?

Jewish tradition teaches that the Ten Plagues successfully destroyed all the false gods of Egypt *except for one* – Baal-zephon. Why? What is it about Baal-zephon that left it unchallenged by all the miraculous signs and wonders that God had done in Egypt?

Who is Baal-zephon?

What is the meaning of the name Baal-zephon? From the prefix *Baal* we know that we are dealing with a pagan god. The biblical text is replete with references to various Baals or pagan gods. *Baal-zevuv*, *Baal-pe'or*, or *Baalim* (the plural of *Baal*) are but a few examples. The Hebrew word *Baal* literally translates as "master", "lord", or "owner." *Zephon* – is the Hebrew word for "north."

A precise translation of *Baal-zephon* is "Master of the North" or "North-Lord."

Remarkably, the Book of the Dead, an ancient Egyptian religious text, mentions a prominent god known as "Lord of the Northern Sky" – an almost perfect translation of the Hebrew

"Baal-zephon." This god's Egyptian name was Set. He was the patron deity of Northern Egypt and was believed to be responsible for fierce desert storms.

According to ancient Egyptian mythology, Set murdered his brother and attempted to kill his nephew Horus. For this, Set was cast out into the lonely desert for eternity. In the 19th Dynasty – the period of Israel's enslavement – there was a resurgence of reverence for Set, and he was seen as a great god, the god who benevolently restrained the forces of the desert and protected Egypt from foreigners.

Desert storms, the sea, and preventing escape?

Set personified the powers of darkness, chaos, and the sea waters that resisted light and order. The prominent 19th-century Egyptologist Dr. Heinrich Brugsch, asserted that, from the standpoint of an Egyptian in Upper Egypt, the north was rightly considered to be the place of darkness, cold, mist, and rain, all of which were attributes of Set; and that the Hebrews called the region of darkness, or the winter hemisphere, Sephon, a name which appears to be connected beyond a doubt with Saphon, "North."

As for Jewish sources, Rabbi Abraham Ibn Ezra (11th century) writes that Baal-zephon was believed to have the power to *prevent slaves from escaping Egypt*.

In light of the above, the tradition that Baal-zephon was the only remaining Egyptian god makes sense. Baal-zephon's dominion was not in Egypt but out *in the desert*. The ten plagues took place in Egypt itself.

Understanding the plan

Let's review the plan:

Speak to the Children of Israel and let them turn back and encamp before Pi-Hahiroth, between Migdol and the sea, before Baal-zephon; you shall encamp opposite it by the sea.

God specifically told Israel to encamp "opposite [Baal-zeph-on] by the sea." Recall that Baal-zephon was believed to control the water.

Pharaoh will say of the Children of Israel 'They are imprisoned [heb. nevuchim] in the land, the desert has locked them in.'

Hearing that Israel were stopped at Baal-zephon, Pharaoh would conclude that Baal-zephon had trapped them. The odd word choice – "They are imprisoned [heb. *nevuchim*] in the land, the desert has locked them in" – can now be explained.

The Hebrew word *nevuchim* is not usually translated as "imprisoned." The actual translation of this word is "perplexed," "depressed," or "confused." One ancient Aramaic translation renders *nevuchim* as *metarfim*, meaning "crazy." (Targum pseudo Jonathan)

If Pharaoh believed that Israel had fallen into the clutches of Baal-zephon – the god responsible for chaos, darkness, and desert storms – describing Israel as *nevuchim* would be an accurate way of saying "Baal-zephon has got them!"

The second phrase in Pharaoh's suggested reaction is *sagar aleihem hamidbar* – "the desert has locked them in." But an equally precise translation would be "he has locked the desert upon them." In other words, Pharaoh believed that Baal-zephon had trapped the children of Israel in the desert.

This understanding is consistent with the ancient Aramaic rendering of Pharaoh's reaction:

"The nation of the House of Israel is crazy in the land, the

god Zephon, master of the desert, has caused them difficulty."
– (Targum ps. Jonathan Exodus 14:3).

Summing up the plan

God led Pharaoh to believe that Baal-zephon had successfully defied the God of Israel. Emboldened by this conclusion, Pharaoh will rush out to defeat Israel in the presence of Baal-zephon, over whom the God of Israel apparently had no power.

Thus, the stage was set for the refutation of the final god of Egypt – and with it all of Egyptian paganism.

With the escaping slaves camped right in front of Baal-zephon, the Egyptian god of storms, chaos, and water was refuted by a storm so orderly that it neatly split the water, miraculously forming two walls. Storms, chaos, and water were all clearly shown to be fully under God's control.

The splitting of the Red Sea is the greatest miracle of the Exodus story not because it was a greater deviation from the laws of nature than, for example, the plague of blood. The splitting of the sea is the greatest miracle—the cause of the great song of praise that Israel sings to God—because through it Egypt and Israel finally and without a shadow of a doubt knew "that I am God."

Yitro

Exodus 18:1-20:23

Making the Sabbath Holy

I N THE COURSE of my work, I frequently conduct Bible studies in Christian churches and seminaries. One of my main goals in these teachings is to sensitize my audience to the precise meaning of the text. Anyone who has heard me teach will be familiar with my constant refrain, "Read the Bible carefully."

It's true that most Christians are unable to read the Bible in the original Hebrew. This shortcoming inevitably hinders their ability to pick up on many of the textual subtleties and anomalies that are worthy of study. That said, by simply reading carefully and asking critical questions, we can gain many insights. And when we ask questions, even if we don't find the answers, we are serving God by exploring His word and seeking the truths within.

One of my favorite examples of the value of reading the Bible carefully is found in the Ten Commandments.

Remember the Sabbath day, to make it holy. Six days you shall labor and do all your work. And the seventh day is Sabbath for the Lord your God: Do not do any work; you and your son and your daughter, your servant and your maidservant and your livestock, and the foreigner within your gates. (Exodus 20:7-9).

A number of questions emerge from a careful reading of this text.

First, we are commanded to "remember the Sabbath day, *to make it holy.*" How is this done? If you were told to make a day holy, what would you do? What exactly is God commanding us to do? We should note that many translations render this phrase: "to keep it holy." This is incorrect. There's no other way to say it. The word *le'kadesho* is clear and simple to translate. It means "to make it holy" or "to sanctify it." The reason these translators opt for "to keep it holy," has nothing to do with actual translation. Rather, they are sensitive to the fact that way back in Genesis 2, we read that "God blessed the seventh day and made it holy," (Genesis 2:3). If God already made the seventh day holy, how can we be commanded to make it holy again? But these translators are missing the point, as I will explain.

A second textual issue relates to the second verse in our passage, "Six days you shall labor and do all your work." What is this verse telling us? Is it a commandment to work for six days? From context we understand that it is setting up the Sabbath. Essentially, it says that, as opposed to the other six days of the week, the Sabbath is a day when we don't work. Still, the plain meaning of the words that seem to command us to work for six days is strange. But a bigger problem with this verse is the second phrase, "and do all your work." This phrase does not appear to add anything of value. If the point of the verse is to tell me that after six days of work, we are to observe the Sabbath, a day when work is forbidden, the verse should have simply said, "Six days you shall labor. And the seventh day is a Sabbath…" What would be missing from our understanding of the commandment to observe the Sabbath if it were written this way? What do the words "and do all your work" add?

Furthermore, within this apparently superfluous phrase, what purpose does the word "all" serve? Why didn't the verse say, "Six days you shall labor and do your work," without the word "all"?

One good rule of thumb when reading the Bible carefully is that if there are words or phrases that appear to be superfluous or redundant, it is precisely those words or phrases that we ought to pay the greatest attention to. These are the words that require greater study. More often than not, it is these seemingly "extra" words that contain the Bible's deepest teachings.

Let's start with the last question we raised. The verse says, "Six days you shall labor and do all your work." What does this even mean? When was the last time you ended a week with "all" your work done? Unless you happened to retire on a Friday, this is impossible. The Jewish sages of 2000 years ago were sensitive to this strange word and commented as follows:

"Is it possible for a person to complete all his work in six days? Rather, [the intent of the verse is] 'Rest on the Sabbath as though all your work is complete.'" (Midrash, Mekhilta, Exodus 9:1:1).

"Rest on the Sabbath *as though all your work is complete.*" In other words, the word "all" teaches us that we are to enter the Sabbath with the frame of mind that "all" our work is done. The Bible is telling us that it is not enough for us not to work on the Sabbath. That would be fine if the sole purpose of the Sabbath were merely to give us a break with a day off. But the Sabbath is meant to be a sanctified day, a day for God. To achieve this, we must put work out of our minds completely.

And in fact, this is exactly what Jews do to this day. Not only is it forbidden to work on the Sabbath, Jewish law forbids us from even discussing work or commerce of any kind. Our financial lives are simply irrelevant. To put a more contemporary spin on this, we shut off our phones, we don't drive our cars, we don't watch TV or use our computers. Once the Sabbath begins, our work is *done*.

Now we can understand the meaning of the entire passage. The first verse states that we must "Remember the Sabbat day to make it holy." We asked how we are supposed to do this? How can people make a day holy? Well, what is holiness? A good definition of holiness is "set aside for God's purposes."

The way we make the Sabbath day holy is spelled out in the verse that follows. "Six days you shall labor and do all your work." In other words, we infuse the day with holiness, ensuring that it is truly set aside for God, by disengaging from our material, financial lives and concerns. This is accomplished by "entering into the Sabbath as though all your work is complete."

The answer to the question of how we are commanded to make the Sabbath holy when God already made it holy is clear and powerful. God, indeed, set aside the seventh day for a higher purpose. He made it holy. But God also created a partnership with Man. Without our cooperation, the Sabbath can lose its holiness. It can be profaned. We are responsible for declaring the holiness of the Sabbath every week. In this way, we align ourselves with His will as Creator.

Although the Sabbath is a commandment to the Jewish people, the nation of Israel, it is also part of the organic makeup of the world. It is part of the created system. To truly experience the holiness of God's day, one day a week, we must disengage from worldly affairs and from our financial, material identities.

Older Christian readers will attest to the fact that in previous generations, Sunday was much more of a Sabbath. Work and commerce were largely absent from the Christian life. Sadly, this is mostly lost. What's more, due to the ubiquitous technology that dominates our lives, the need to disengage from worldly affairs to properly honor God is needed more than ever before.

As any Shabbat-observant Jew will tell you, disengagement from media and work through shutting off our phones, not driving anywhere, and not engaging in commerce leads to increased engagement with family and community. With nobody going anywhere, nobody on their phones, and nobody focused on work, families and communities spend time together, worshiping, studying, and simply enjoying real relationships. Now more than ever, we need the Sabbath in our lives.

Mishpatim

Exodus 21:1-24:18

Sapphire and the Kingdom of Heaven

A FTER THE REVELATION at Mount Sinai, where God spoke the Ten Commandments to the nation of Israel, this week's Bible portion opens with two chapters of laws (Exodus 22-23) spoken by God to Moses at that time. Then, in chapter 24, the Bible tells us that Moses relayed these laws to the people (Exodus 24:3). Moses then wrote the words of the law, built an altar, offered sacrifices to God, and sprinkled some of the blood on the people as a sign of the covenant (v.4-8). And then we read the following:

> *Moses and Aaron, Nadav and Avihu, and seventy of the elders of Israel went up. They saw the God of Israel, and under His feet was like a configuration of sapphire brick, and it was like the very heavens in purity. (Exodus 24:9-10).*

What exactly happened in this scene is unclear. Moses, Aaron, Aaron's sons, and the elders of Israel experienced a prophetic vision. That much is clear. But how do we understand what they saw? Does God have feet? And what does "like a configuration of sapphire brick" mean? What is the meaning of this vision?

Sapphire appears in two other prophecies in the Bible. Isaiah 54 is a prophecy spoken by Isaiah to the city of Jerusalem. Speaking to the holy city, Isaiah comforts Jerusalem by describing the future rebuilding of the city in the End Times. In that context, Isaiah prophesies that Jerusalem's foundations will be laid with sapphire.

Afflicted and stormed-tossed one, who has not been comforted. Behold I will set your flagstones with carbuncle and lay your foundations with sapphire. – Isaiah 54:11

The other prophetic vision involving sapphire is in Ezekiel. Chapter 1 of Ezekiel is one of the most difficult-to-understand passages in the Bible. It describes the "chariot," or throne of God. In this vision, Ezekiel saw God sitting – so to speak – on His throne of glory.

Above the firmament that was over their heads was the likeness of a throne, like the appearance of a sapphire stone; and upon the likeness of the throne was a likeness, like the appearance of a person on it from above. (Ezekiel 1:26).

To sum up. Our verse here in Exodus 24 describes a vision "like a configuration of sapphire brick" under the feet of God in the wake of receiving the law at Sinai. Isaiah prophesies that the foundations of Jerusalem of the future will be made of sapphire. In Ezekiel's vision of God sitting on His throne, the throne is made of sapphire.

Sapphire is a beautiful gemstone. Although it can appear in a variety of colors, including colorless, its most common color is sky-blue. Like many gems, sapphire is transparent like glass. To describe something as "like sapphire" is to say that it is beautiful, sky-blue, and transparent.

When we say that an object is transparent, we are describing that its inside and outside are simultaneously visible. For a transparent object, it's difficult to tell where the outside ends and the inside begins. On the other hand, an object that is not transparent can not be seen on the inside by looking at the outer surface. The internal nature is concealed by the opaque outer layer.

God is the creator and sustainer of all things. The inner purpose of everything in creation is the glory of God. The goal of life, according to the Bible is to see God in everything. Unfortunately, this isn't how we experience the world on a day-to-day basis. When we look at the world around us, the internal essence and purpose of creation is not readily apparent to our senses. We don't easily see Godliness in all things. Our vision is obscured by the dark outer layer of reality.

When practiced properly, the laws of the Bible sensitize us to God's presence all around us. A life of obedience to God's law allows us to see God. For example, when I praise God before and after I eat, the experience of eating becomes about so much more than the taste, texture, and nutritional value of the food. By reminding myself that the food I am eating was created for me by God, I experience the Godliness inherent in the food.

The goal of the entire Bible, the goal of a life of faith and service of God, is to make everything like sapphire. With the Bible as our guide, everything in creation speaks of God's beauty and reminds us of the heavens. More importantly, everything becomes transparent, meaning that the inner essence and purpose – the glory of God – becomes visible. Like sapphire, external material existence and its internal Godly essence become indistinguishable.

So when Isaiah said that the foundations of Jerusalem of the future will be sapphire, he meant this: Jerusalem, the capital city of the kingdom of God on earth, will be a place where the beauty and Godliness inherent in everything are visible and tangible.

This same idea is expressed by Ezekiel's vision of God's throne. Kings sit on thrones. God is all-powerful. God is the creator and ruler. This is true in all times and places, whether or not people recognize Him. But when the Bible refers to God as king, it means something more specific. Consider this verse in Zechariah, one of many verses that convey this idea.

The Lord will be king over the whole earth. On that day there will be one Lord, and his name the only name. (Zechariah 14:9)

The Lord *will* be king…? Isn't He already king? When the Bible refers to God as king, it means much more than the fact that God is the supreme ruler. It means that people recognize Him as such. So, when Zechariah said that "the Lord will be king," he meant that everyone would know Him and serve Him. When Ezekiel described God's throne as made of sapphire, he was telling us that God's kingship is all about what sapphire represents, seeing the inner heavenly truth of the earthly material world.

Let's return to our verse in Exodus 24. Recall that this vision occurred immediately after the children of Israel received God's law at Sinai. The vision of Moses, Aaron, his sons, and the elders is described as "like a configuration of sapphire brick." In the original Hebrew, this phrase is *kema'aseh livnat hasapir*, which literally translates to "like the work of the brick of sapphire."

I'd like to suggest that this vision was a description of the covenant itself.

After spending generations making bricks in Egypt, the children of Israel are told that they have a new task. They will no longer make bricks for Pharaoh. Their new construction project is to build the kingdom of God "under His feet" in the lower, material world. They are to build a world in which God's presence, the inner essence of everything, is tangible and perceptible. This work is "the work of the brick of sapphire."

Terumah

Exodus 25:1-27:19

Cherubs – Our Interface with God

S EVERAL PORTIONS OF the Bible are dedicated to discussing the construction of the sanctuary, including the collecting of materials for and building of the Tabernacle, the portable temple that the children of Israel built in the desert, and everything in it. These sections do not describe the actual collecting and building. In this portion, -d dictates the details of this project to Moshe.

One of the central items in the Tabernacle is the Ark of the Covenant. The ark was a box made of cedar wood and gold. Its function was to house the two tablets of the covenant that Moses brought down from Mount Sinai. The following verses describe the cover of the ark.

"Make a cover of pure gold, two and one-half cubits long and one and one-half cubits wide. Make two golden Cherubim [plural of cherub]. You must make them by hammering them out of the two ends of the cover. Make one Cherub out of one end and one Cherub out of the other end. From the [same piece of gold as the] cover itself, you shall make the

Cherubim on its two ends. The Cherubim shall spread their wings upward, sheltering the cover with their wings, and the Cherubim shall face one another. Their faces shall be inclined toward the cover [i.e. facing down]. Place the cover on top of the ark and place the testimony [i.e. the tablets] that I will give you into the ark. I will meet with you there and I will speak with you from above the cover – from between the Cherubim that are on the ark of the testimony – all that which I will command you concerning the Children of Israel." (Exodus 25:17-22).

The two Cherubs were to be hammered out of the same piece of gold as the cover itself. They were not to be made separately and then soldered onto the cover. The cherubs were made to be standing facing each other, their faces pointing down toward the box and their wings raised upward. God's word would then come to Moses from between the two Cherubim.

What are Cherubim? What is their purpose? What do they symbolize? What do they have to do with prophecy? Why was it necessary to make them out of the same piece of gold as the rest of the cover of the ark?

What is a Cherub?

The first appearance of Cherubs in the Bible occurs when God banished Adam and Eve from the Garden of Eden for having sinned. "He banished Adam, and at the east of the Garden of Eden He stationed the Cherubim and the flame of the rotating sword to guard the way to the Tree of Life." (Genesis 4:24).

From this passage, we see that the role of Cherubs is to guard and protect.

Cherubs appear in this role in a number of biblical texts (see Ezekiel 28:14).

Besides serving as guards and protectors, we also see Cherubs in the Bible serving as the "vehicle" or seat of God's presence. Numerous Biblical texts refer to -d as "the One who dwells on [or rides] the Cherubim." Here are a few examples:

"And He rides the Cherub and flies off" (Psalms 18:11)

Now the glory of the God of Israel went up from above the cherubim, where it had been, and moved to the threshold of the temple. (Ezekiel 9:3)

He rode upon a cherub, and flew, and He [d]was seen upon the wings of the wind (2 Samuel 22:11)

Rabbi Samson Raphael Hirsch (19th century Germany) asserts that the Cherubim atop the ark filled both of the roles we just mentioned. They protected and guarded, and at the same time they served as the vehicle and seat of God's presence. This dual role writes Rabbi Hirsch, is apparent from the description of the wings of the Cherubim. He explains this as follows:

The verse states that "The Cherubim shall spread their wings upward," i.e. they continually reach toward heaven. In this way, they represent the spiritual rise toward God, a continual "reaching upward." At the same time, the Cherubim are described as "sheltering the cover with their wings." The same wings that serve as the vehicle for Godliness serve to guard and protect the Tablets of the Testimony – the Bible. The dual purpose of the Cherubim is to carry – to serve as the vehicle for – that which is above and to protect that which is below.

I would like to suggest a slightly different interpretation of Rabbi Hirsch's interpretation of the Cherubim's wings.

The verse describes the posture and position of the Cherubim as follows:

The Cherubim shall spread their wings upward, sheltering the cover with their wings, and the Cherubim shall face one another. Their faces shall be inclined toward the cover.

Let's sum this up. The wings were raised in such as manner as to shelter the cover of the ark. The faces of the Cherubs were facing each other but inclined downward. Picture a bird in this position, face pointed at the ground with wings raised in a manner that hovers over the ground below. This is not the posture of a bird taking flight. Rather, what is described is how a bird looks when it is landing.

To understand the significance of this, let's turn our attention to the cover of the ark.

The verse states: "From the [same piece of gold as the] cover itself, you shall make the Cherubim." Why not simply make them separately and attach the completed Cherubs to the golden cover? Why add this seemingly useless difficulty to the process?

As mentioned above, one of the purposes of the Cherubim was to protect the contents of the ark – the Bible. This role can be filled perfectly well by the cover without the Cherubs. A simple cover would surely provide protection. It would seem that the Cherubs are not necessary for the protection of the ark. The instruction to fashion the Cherubs out of the same piece of gold as the cover teaches that we must not differentiate. The Cherubs and the cover are one and the same. To speak of the cover without the Cherubs is impossible.

Think about it. The Cherubs had the dual role of protecting the ark's contents and serving as the "seat" of God's glory, the place where God's word entered into this world. This is why the

Cherubs were fashioned in such a way as to depict them landing rather than flying off. The Cherubs represented the descent of God's presence into this world.

The message of the Cherubs is powerful and relevant to all people of Biblical faith. We must protect and guard the Bible. Protecting and guarding the Bible is how we bring God's presence into this world and create a throne for God down here on earth. The two tasks are indistinguishable.

Tetzaveh

Exodus 27:20-30:10

Revealing God in the Tabernacle

T HE PORTION OF the Bible called Tetzaveh makes up the second
half of the instructions for the construction of the Tabernacle.
From a narrative perspective, these two Bible portions (Terumah and
Tetzaveh) constitute one continuous prophecy to Moses. The portion
titled Terumah, which is read the week before Tetzaveh, begins with
the words, "And the Lord spoke to Moses saying." (Exodus 25:1)
From that point until the end of Tetzaveh which is more than four
chapters, and concludes with Exodus 30:10, we find no interruption
in God's words to Moses. Only when we reach the opening verse
of Exodus 30:11, do we again see the words, "And the Lord spoke
to Moses saying," indicating a new unit of prophecy.

This leads to the question: what accounts for the division of
the two portions of the Bible from one week to the next? Were
they divided simply to break up a long section into two parts
for the sake of convenience because we don't want the portions
to be too long? Is there any thematic rationale behind the specific point at which they were divided?

The portion of Terumah began with the words, "And the Lord

spoke to Moses saying." (25:1). Interestingly, the appearance of God's name in this verse is the only time God is mentioned by any name in that portion. Now, at first glance, this may not seem so strange. After all, God Himself is speaking continuously for the entire portion. It would make sense that He doesn't mention His own name.

The problem with this line of thinking is that, as I mentioned above, these two portions of the Bible are one continuous monologue by God to Moses. After God's name does not appear even once for 95 consecutive verses in Terumah, Tetzaveh mentions God's name, Adonai—"The Lord"- 23 times. The name Elohim—"God"—appears three times as well.

To sum up, even though these two weekly Bible portions constitute one continuous prophetic monologue by God, His name does not appear in the content of what God said in Terumah even once. And then, in this week's portion, God mentions Himself by name 26 times.

To help us understand the significance and message of the difference between these two portions, let's take a look at the content.

Here is a list, in order, of the instructions given to Moses over these two Bible portions.

Terumah (Exodus 25:1-27:19)
1. Call for donations – (25:1-9)
2. The Ark – (25:10-22)
3. The Table – (25:23-30)
4. The Menorah – (25:31-40)
5. Coverings for the roof of the Tabernacle – (26:1-14)
6. Tabernacle walls – (26:15-37)
7. The altar for burnt offerings – (27:1-8)
8. The Tabernacle courtyard – (27:9-19)

Tetzaveh (Exodus 27:20-30:10)

1. Instructions for lighting the Menorah – (27:20-21)
2. Preparation of priestly vestments – (28:1-43)
3. Instructions for sacrificial offerings of the investiture of Aaron and his sons – (29:1-37)
4. Instructions for the daily offering – (29:38-46)
5. The incense altar, including the daily offering of incense – (30:1-10)

One of the first things we notice is the separation between the crafting of the Menorah, appearing in the opening chapter of Terumah, and the lighting of the Menorah, which begins in Tetzaveh.

Using this one detail as a guide, we can see the significant thematic difference between these two portions.

Terumah dealt with the construction of the Tabernacle and its key objects, while Tetzaveh dealt with the service performed in the Tabernacle.

Let me put this another way. Tetzaveh describes the living, breathing, active life of the Tabernacle on a day-to-day basis. The priests, their clothing, the lighting of the Menorah, sacrificial offerings, all these are descriptions of the activity that took place in the Tabernacle, not the structure of it. The incense altar is the only vessel whose construction is included in this portion. While there are many answers given as to why it is mentioned here, it is clearly the exception that proves the rule.

Unlike the Menorah, which was lit only at night, there was always incense on the incense altar. Incense was offered on the altar both first thing in the morning and then again at the end of the day to burn at night. Incense burned on the altar at all times (see Exodus 30:7-8). I'd like to suggest that this is the reason the incense altar is mentioned here. It was the only one of the objects in the Tabernacle that was in continuous use. In other words, there is no incense altar without the service of incense. The incense altar did not exist independently of the worship upon it.

If we sum up the points we have made thus far, the emerging message is clear and relevant to our lives.

Last week's Bible portion was about the structure and items contained within the Tabernacle. This portion does not mention God by name.

This week's Bible portion is about the priests and the daily service in the Tabernacle. God's name appears throughout.

Terumah was about the structure of the Tabernacle. Tetzaveh is about the living content within the Tabernacle.

Our life of faith, like the Tabernacle and the eventual Temple in Jerusalem, includes both outer structure and inner life. We build and maintain synagogues and churches. As Jews, we purchase and build ritual objects to be used in service of God. But God's name is not to be found in buildings and objects. God's name, His Presence, is revealed when we serve Him.

A beautiful Tabernacle, synagogue, or church building does not reveal the presence of God. The candlesticks used to light Shabbat candles each week and the Bible scrolls in the ark in the synagogue do not reveal the name and presence of God. When living, breathing human beings worship Him, when we *light* the Shabbat candles, when we *read* from the Bible scroll. That is how God's name appears.

At the very beginning of Terumah, when introducing the concept of a Tabernacle, or Temple. God said,

And they shall make for me a sanctuary, and I will dwell among them (Exodus 25:8).

God did not say, "and I will dwell in it," referring to the Tabernacle. Rather, "I will dwell among them" within the people of Israel. God does not dwell in houses of worship. He dwells in the worshippers.

Ki Tisa

Exodus 30:11-34:35

The Cast Calf

*And the people gathered around Aaron and said to him, "Arise!
Make for us gods that will go before us, for this man Moses who
brought us up from the land of Egypt – we do not know what
became of him." Aaron said to them, "Remove the rings of gold
that are in the ears of your wives, sons, and daughters, and bring
them to me." The entire people removed the gold rings that were
in their ears and brought them to Aaron. He took it from their
hand, fashioned it with an engraving tool and made it into a calf
of cast metal [Heb. masechah]. They said, "These are your gods,
Israel, who brought you up from the land of Egypt!"*

*God spoke to Moses: "Go descend, for your people that you
have brought up from the land of Egypt has become corrupt.
They have turned aside very quickly from the path that I have
commanded them; they have made themselves a calf of cast
metal! [masechah]" (Exodus 32:1-4,7-8)*

THE BIBLE PORTION titled Ki Tisa is dominated by the story
of the sin of the Golden Calf. In describing both the sin and

God's reaction to it, the Bible mentions the method of making the calf – that it was *cast metal*. Notice that God did not mention the fact that it was gold. Apparently, the fact that the calf was cast was of greater significance to God than the fact that it was gold.

At the end of this narrative, God relayed a series of laws to Moses, including the following – an obvious reaction to the sin of the calf:

You shall not make for yourselves gods of cast metal. (34:17).

Forty years after this sin, in the book of Deuteronomy, Moses recounted many of the events of the sojourn in the desert. Here is Moses' retelling of God's initial reaction to the Golden Calf:

God said to me, "Arise! Go down quickly from here because your people has corrupted – whom you took out of Egypt. They have turned aside very quickly from the path that I have commanded them; they have made themselves a cast metal image [masechah]]!" (Deuteronomy 9:12).

Remarkably, not only does Moses omit the fact that the calf was gold. He doesn't even mention the fact that it was a calf. The only description he gives of it is that it was cast! From all this it is clear that God was angered primarily at the fact that they had made a cast metal image. The fact that it was a calf – or golden – is of secondary importance!

Why? What is the importance of cast metal that makes it so central to this sin?

The Hebrew word for cast metal used in all these verses is ma-SE-kha. This word has variant meanings. It sometimes means "a mask" or "a cover" (see Isaiah 25:7, 20). Ma-SE-kha can also mean "leader" or "anointed one" (Isaiah 30:1, according to biblical commentary on this verse. This last meaning is a secondary meaning based on the verb "to pour," which is also used to describe anointing with oil and offering a libation, both of which involve pouring. To sum up this point, the word *masecha*, which means "cast metal," is from the root "to pour."

Ma-SE-kha – cast metal – is metal that is poured. It is melted down into liquid and then poured into a mold or onto a three-dimensional form. The reason that it is also the word for "mask" is likely due to the fact that a mask is an empty form, similar to a mold for casting.

That the Bible places great importance on how an object is fashioned should not be surprising. The instructions for the building of the Tabernacle are full of specific instructions regarding the methods of manufacturing particular items. For example, the altar may not be made of hewn stone due to using a metal blade or sharp object to cut the stone. In the words of the Bible, "for if you have wielded your sword over it, you will have desecrated it." (Exodus 20:22).

The two objects made of pure gold – the Cherubs and the Menorah – also have specific instructions. Each of these items was required to be made out of a solid piece of gold. Also, each of these items had to be smithed – not cast (see Exodus 25:18, 25:31). Smithing is the process of shaping a piece of metal by hammering and beating it into shape. Smithing is a much more difficult and time-consuming method of making these two items than casting would be. Both the Cherubs and the Menorah required a great deal of fine detail work. It certainly would have been quicker and easier to make a wax mold of the Menorah, melt down the gold, and cast it. Nevertheless, the Bible requires smithing – not casting. Why?

As I stated above, smithing is a very slow process. It takes time and precision. Casting happens fast, especially with gold, which cools and hardens very quickly. All that is needed to create a cast object is to heat up the gold and pour it into the mold. But, you might be wondering, doesn't it take time to create the mold or form that the molten metal is poured into? The answer is yes if that's how the casting is being done. But there is another way to cast an object, and it appears that this was the method used to make the Golden Calf.

The entire people removed the gold rings that were in their ears and brought them to Aaron. He took it from their hand, fashioned it with an engraving tool, and made it into a calf of cast metal.

If Aaron was casting the calf, why did he need an engraving tool? Doesn't casting involve simply pouring the liquid gold into the mold? The answer is yes if you have time to make a detailed mold. Another way to cast gold, due to how fast it cools and how soft it is as a metal, is to create a crude mold that approximates the final object's shape, pour the liquid gold into it, and then manipulate the soft, cooling gold as it hardens using a tool to shape it.

Many years ago, I spoke to a friend who worked in the precious metals refining business. I asked him how he would have made the Golden Calf. He said that creating a detailed mold of a calf out there in the desert would have taken too much time. He said he would dig a hole in the ground with four legs to approximate the shape of the body of a calf, melt the gold, pour it in, and then shape it quickly as it was cooling. I'd like to suggest that this is precisely what the verses here describe.

Israel made the Golden Calf because they felt a need for a physical representation of God's presence. They were not trying to replace God. This is why they said of the calf,

These are your gods, Israel, who brought you up from the land of Egypt! (Exodus 32:4).

They saw the calf as a vessel that would now house God – the same God who took them out of Egypt. The problem with this is that God can not be housed in any physical object. God can not take any physical form whatsoever. For this reason, drawing or fashioning physical representations of God is forbidden.

Liquid has no form of its own. Liquid takes the physical form of whatever vessel it is in. In the absence of a vessel, it will expand and flow endlessly. In casting, liquid metal is given a specific form according to the mold into which it is poured. Casting provides a perfect metaphor for the theological mistake made by those who made the Golden Calf. Godlike liquid – has no physical form. To create an outside form and "pour" God into it – to cast God – is heretical. God fills all of creation and can not be restricted or housed by a particular object.

But there is another lesson in the difference between smithing and casting. As mentioned, the two solid gold items in the Tabernacle, the Menorah, and the Cherubs, were smithed even though making them by casting would certainly have been much quicker and easier.

I believe that the lesson here is profound. Neither of these objects represented God. The Cherubs represent our interface with God as His spirit enters the world. The Cherubs sat atop the Ark that housed the tablets representing the covenant at Sinai. The Cherubs represent our protecting of the law through our service of God. The Menorah represents the light that we must bring into the world.

The insistence on smithing these items teaches us a critical lesson for our lives of faith. Casting, as opposed to smithing, happens fast through the application of fire. This represents the kind of sudden passion and emotional momentum that is inappropriate for serving God with integrity. While we certainly experience moments of sudden inspiration, and spiritual high points where we feel close to God, these moments are not what a life of service to God is built on. We don't experience Mount Sinai or the splitting of the sea on a daily basis. How often have we seen or experienced, how sudden spiritual highs can be so fleeting, often leaving us feeling depressed when we realize days or years later that we have retained little of that momentary inspiration?

For our service of God to be lasting and meaningful in the long term, it must be built on deliberate, careful work, day after day. A life of faith requires effort, commitment, and consistency. Smithing is the way to serve God, not casting.

Vaykhel
Exodus 35:1-38:20

All Are Equal in the
House of God

T HE PORTION OF the Bible Vayakhel describes the construction of the Tabernacle, the portable temple constructed in
the desert. But before the construction could begin, they first
needed to collect all the materials necessary for the Tabernacle
structure: the ark, the menorah, the incense, spices, oil, the vessels, curtains, and priestly garments. The Bible tells us that the
people generously donated these materials.

> *Moses said to the whole community of Israel, "This is what
> the Lord has commanded: Take from what you have an of-
> fering for the Lord. Anyone generous of heart is to bring an
> offering of God, of gold, silver and bronze; blue, purple and
> scarlet yarn and fine linen; goat hair; ram skins dyed red and
> tachash skins; acacia wood; olive oil for the light; spices for
> the anointing oil and for the fragrant incense; and onyx stones
> and other gems to be mounted on the ephod and breastpiece."
> Exodus 35:4-9).*

After listing everything to be constructed (verses 10-19), the Bible tells us that the people generously gave all that was needed.

All the Israelite men and women whose hearts were generous brought all that was needed for the work the Lord had commanded them to do through Moses; the children of Israel brought freewill gifts to the Lord. (Exodus 35:29).

The generosity of the people is emphasized by the extra phrase at the end of this verse, "the children of Israel brought freewill gifts to the Lord." Anyone who has ever been involved in a fundraising campaign for a large project knows how unusual it is for a project's needs to be donated with such ease. The generosity of the children of Israel was so great that they kept giving even after everything necessary had been raised. As we read a few verses later:

And the people continued to bring freewill offerings every morning. So, all the skilled workers who were doing all the work on the sanctuary left what they were doing and came forward. They said to Moses, "The people are bringing more than enough for doing the work the Lord commanded to be done." Then Moses gave an order, and they sent this word throughout the camp, saying, "No man or woman is to make anything else as an offering for the sanctuary." And so the people were restrained from bringing more. What they already had was more than enough to do all the work. Exodus 36:4-7).

The Bible goes on to tell us in great detail what was made from each donated material. But not everything made in the Tabernacle was made from materials donated during this fundraising campaign. Allow me to explain.

As I mentioned, the Tabernacle was a portable temple that

traveled with the people of Israel during the 40 years in the desert. It was made to be taken apart, transported, and reassembled. The walls of the Tabernacle were made of beams of acacia wood. Each beam was 10 cubits long and one and a half cubits wide. There were 48 wooden beams in total. The walls were put together by lining up he beam vertically, side by side. Each beam would be mounted in 2 silver bases or sockets. The end of each beam had two protruding pieces that would each lock into a silver socket. The beams were then connected horizontally with crossbeams.

Outside the central Tabernacle structure was the courtyard, which was enclosed by a curtain mounted on beams. This curtain was fastened to the beams with silver hooks.

Unlike the materials used for everything else in the Tabernacle, the silver used for these hooks and the bases for the wood beams did not come from "anyone of generous heart." The source of this silver was not the fundraising campaign we read about here in chapter 35. Later on, in chapter 38, we read:

And the silver from those who were numbered of the congregation was one hundred talents and one thousand seven hundred and seventy-five shekels, according to the shekel of the sanctuary: ... And from the hundred talents of silver were cast the sockets of the sanctuary and the bases of the curtain: one hundred sockets from the hundred talents, one talent for each socket. Then, from the one thousand seven hundred and seventy-five shekels he made hooks for the pillars, overlaid their capitals, and made bands for them. (Exodus 38:25,27-28)

Back in Exodus 30, we read that a census of Israel was taken. The way they counted the census was for each person over the age of 20 to give a half shekel of silver, no more and no less. As we read there:

Everyone included among those who are numbered, from twenty years old and above, shall give an offering to the Lord. The rich shall not give more, and the poor shall not give less than half a shekel, when you give an offering to the Lord, to make atonement for yourselves. – Exodus 30:14-15

"The silver from those who were numbered of the congregation" here in Exodus 35 refers to the census in Exodus 30. The use of the silver of the census for the sockets and hooks contains a powerful lesson. There were certainly those among the children of Israel who were wealthier and those who were poorer. Obviously, those who had more were able to give more. It is the responsibility of those who are blessed with greater wealth to give more to communal needs. This was as true then as it is today. But there is a downside. It is only natural that those who are wealthy and have contributed more to the public needs, say, building a synagogue or church, will feel a greater sense of ownership and propriety over the finished product. Someone in the community who cannot afford to give could easily feel that the temple or church they attend for worship is not really theirs, that they are merely guests, worshiping through the goodwill of the wealthier members of the community.

The half shekel of silver that everyone was required to give solved this problem. As mentioned, the rich could not give more, the poor could not give less. All were equal in the half shekel donation. Then, these very same half-shekels were melted down and used as the base sockets and hooks that held the entire structure of the Tabernacle together.

The message is clear. Without the equally valuable contribution of each and every member of the community, there is no Tabernacle. It cannot stand. All are equally needed to build and uphold God's house.

In later years, the half shekel was collected every year as well. These shekels were used for the communal offerings brought daily and on the festivals throughout the year. The message was the same. When an offering is brought in the Temple on behalf of the community of Israel, all are represented equally. The community of God must include everyone.

Pekudei
Exodus 38:21-40:38

The Ongoing Revelation
at Sinai

THE FINAL BIBLE portion of Exodus concludes with the erecting of the Tabernacle.

The Bible states, "And Moses erected the Tabernacle." (Exodus 40:18). The fifteen verses that follow detail every aspect of the setup of the Tabernacle and everything it. What is striking about this lengthy description is the emphasis on Moses himself. The singular verbs clearly imply that this work was done entirely by Moses. For example:

> *Moses erected the tabernacle, fastened its sockets, set up its boards, put in its bars, and erected its pillars. He spread out the tent over the tabernacle and put the covering of the tent over it from above, as the Lord had commanded Moses. He took the Testimony and put it into the ark, inserted the poles through the rings of the ark, and put the ark-cover on top of the ark. (Exodus 40:18-20).*

On and on, the text continues in this fashion, in the third person singular, for 15 verses. As if to emphasize that it was Moses alone who did all the work, the passage concludes with this verse:

He erected the courtyard around the Tabernacle and the altar
and put up the screen of the gate of the courtyard; Moses con-
cluded the labor (Exodus 40:33).

Whether Moses alone actually did all the work, such as moving furniture and vessels, erecting the many large wooden beams, and building the courtyard, or if he is being credited for the job because he was the leader, is a speculative question worth pondering. For our purposes as readers of the Bible, we must ask a more basic question: Why? Why does the Bible emphasize Moses as the sole constructor of the Tabernacle? What lesson can we derive from this?

To answer this question, let's explore another, more fundamental question regarding the Tabernacle. What was its purpose? Why was it set up just the way it was?

The great commentator and rabbinic leader Rabbi Moses Nachmanides (13th century France), known by the acronym Ramban, maintains that the Tabernacle, and the temple in Jerusalem after it, served as an extension of the revelatory experience of the giving of the Bible at Mount Sinai.

As we read in Exodus 19, at Sinai, the children of Israel surrounded the mountain. There were boundaries beyond which the people were forbidden to pass. There was an inner boundary into which only the priests were allowed and the point of contact with God was in the center. At that point of contact with God, the voice of God was heard, and Moses was given the law in the form of the two tablets of the covenant. Moreover, as the Bible tells us, there was smoke rising from the mountain.

Similarly, with regard to the setup of the camp of Israel in the desert, the nation camped around the Tabernacle; there was an inner boundary for the Levites and priests. The people were not allowed into the inner part of the Tabernacle. At the innermost point of the Tabernacle was the Ark of the Covenant, containing the two tablets of the law given at Sinai. Atop the ark sat the Cherubs, the point of contact with God, the entry point of God's prophetic word into the world. Finally, the burning of incense day and night produced a pillar of smoke that rose from the sanctuary, a few feet away from the Ark. Therefore, through the presence of the Tabernacle, the revelation at Sinai was experienced in perpetuity.

All of this can be equally applied to the temple in Jerusalem, which is geographically located in the center of the land of Israel, with the tribes of Israel surrounding it on all sides.

It is clear from this arrangement that the epicenter of the Tabernacle was the Ark of the Covenant. This was the only item in the innermost chamber, the Holy of Holies, which even the High Priest was only allowed to enter under very limited circumstances. As mentioned, the Ark, situated in the Holy of Holies, contained the tablets.

Once again, the ark contained the tablets of the law and was covered by the Cherubs, which the Bible tells us was the entry point for God's prophetic word. What does this mean? Simply put, it means that the covenant of the law represented by the tablets served as the basis for prophecy, the highest point of contact between God and man.

There is a powerful lesson here that we must understand. In the minds of many people of faith, the primary encounter with God is through prayer and worship. Prayer is certainly an essential component of our relationship with God. As Jews, we pray three times a day. When there was a Tabernacle or Temple, the primary form of worship was the sacrificial offerings. But notice the setup of the Tabernacle.

The sacrifices were offered in the *outer* area, not in the holy or holy of holies. In other words, the purpose of prayer and worship is to draw us closer to God. In fact, the Hebrew word for "sacrifice," *korban*, literally means "that which draws close." But our primary purpose and mission as servants of God is not prayer or the offering of sacrifices. Prayer and sacrifices, worship, is a means to an end. The most important way that we serve God is by carrying out His will on this earth.

Let me put this another way. When we pray to God, we are trying to get Him to do our will. When we study His word and obediently carry out His commands, we align our will with His. The purpose of sacrifices and worship is to draw us closer to Him so that we will ultimately embrace our mission, to serve Him by doing His work in the world. That mission is contained in the Bible and in the prophetic word of God, represented by the Ark of the Covenant.

Moses was not the High Priest. It might have made more sense to us that if anyone should be putting the Tabernacle together all by himself, it should be Aaron, not Moses. But Moses was the greatest prophet and, more importantly, Moses was the one who relayed the Bible, God's law and mission, to the children of Israel.

In many religious systems, prayer is the primary experience of a relationship with God. In Judaism, it is the Bible. Bible study brings a person to an understanding of the will of God. When one understands a particular verse or Bible idea, one is communing with God on the most intimate level. One is blending his thoughts with God's thoughts, so to speak. In this experience, the will of God and our will become synonymous. It is a blending of our very identities with the Divine.

In prayer, I stand *before* God. In Bible study, I am *with* Him. More importantly, in fulfillment of the Bible, I become God's agent, carrying out His will in the world.

Moses, the giver of the Bible, fully erected the Tabernacle, with the Bible at its center, to emphasize the primacy of Bible wisdom and practice as the most intimate connection to God.

As the Ramban compared the setup of the Tabernacle in the camp to the revelation at Sinai, so too can this idea be seen in the setup of the Jewish People in the land of Israel. Jerusalem, the epicenter of our encounter with God, sits in the middle of the country, while Jerusalem itself is surrounded by the camp of Israel.

Even as we turn *towards* Jerusalem in prayer, we must also open our minds and hearts to hear the message that is coming *from* Jerusalem. Ultimately, the surest way for God to dwell within our midst is through the study and practice of Bible.

"For from Tzion shall go forth Bible and the word of Hashem from Jerusalem." Isaiah 2:3).

Leviticus

Vayikra
Leviticus 1:1-5:26

Yeast, Honey, and Salt

THE EARLY CHAPTERS of Leviticus discuss the various sacrifices and offerings to be brought to the Tabernacle and, after
entering Israel, the Temple in Jerusalem. At the end of the discussion of the meal offering, the following rules are stated.

> *"All meal offerings that you bring to God are not to be made
> leavened, for all yeast [heb. se'or – alt. trans. 'sourdough' or
> 'leaven'] and all honey you shall not burn from them a fire-of-
> fering to God. You shall bring them as a first [fruit-] offering
> to God but they shall not be placed upon the altar as a pleas-
> ing fragrance. You shall salt all your meal-offerings with salt
> and you shall not omit salt from [being placed] upon your
> meal-offerings. On all your offerings, you shall bring salt."
> (Leviticus. 2:11-13).*

The above passage relates to three laws. No leavened offerings
are to be brought, no honey is to be included in any offering,
and all offerings must include salt.

Maimonides (12th century), in *The Guide of the Perplexed*

(section III, chapters 45-46), asserts that many of the laws regarding sacrifices were commanded to contradict and counteract the beliefs and practices of idolatry. Maimonides' comment on the above passage from Leviticus—consistent with his overall approach—follows.

> *"Inasmuch as the idolaters offered only leavened bread and made many offerings of sweet things and seasoned their sacrifices with honey, as is generally recognized in the books that I have mentioned to you, and thus no salt was to be found in any of their offerings, He, may He be exalted, forbade offering up any leaven or any honey and commanded that salt always be offered: 'with all thine offerings thou shalt offer salt'"* (Guide III, 46).

Maimonides' comment is certainly interesting as an answer to the basic question of why we are so commanded. That said, his comment leads us to another more fundamental question. Why did the pagans bring leavened sacrifices and honey-sweetened sacrifices? Why did they refrain from including salt in any of their offerings? What is the theological point of these idolatrous practices – a point that is being rejected by the Bible?

Leaven plays an important role in Jewish practice, most notably by its omission on Passover. The Bible forbids the eating of leaven on Passover because our ancestors ate unleavened bread in Egypt. Furthermore, the Passover offering is required to be eaten together with unleavened bread. Does it really matter that our ancestors ate unleavened bread in Egypt? They probably ate a lot of other things that we do not commemorate as well. If they had somehow managed to leaven their bread, would that fact change the important details of the Exodus story?

Consider the difference between unleavened and leavened

bread. They have the same basic ingredients – flour and water. The difference between them is that the unleavened bread did not have time to rise. In fact, *matzah* – the unleavened bread that we eat on Passover - is considered leavened and unkosher for Passover if it is not baked within eighteen minutes from the time the water comes into contact with the flour. *Matzah* is rushed and undeveloped. It is uncomplicated. Leaven takes its sweet time. Baking bread is one of the most time-consuming processes of all food preparation. A slave can not take the time to bake his own bread.

Matza, unleavened bread, symbolizes the idea of humility and simplicity. All meal offerings in the temple must be unleavened because these are the traits with which we must come before God.

Salt and honey are both flavor enhancers. However, the ways that they enhance flavor could not be more different. Honey doesn't actually enhance the flavor of the food it is added to. It merely adds the flavor of honey. Like the line from Mary Poppins, "A spoon full of sugar helps the medicine go down," honey and sugar simply mask the flavor of the other food with the addition of sweetness. Salt, on the other hand, rather than masking flavor, actually enhances the flavor of the food to which it is added. Salt draws out flavors from other foods. A related quality of salt is that is draws out the inner essence of whatever it is added to. For example, raw meat, when salted, will secrete blood stored inside it.

To sum up this point: Honey enhances flavor by masking it. Salt enhances flavor by drawing out more of the essence of the food to which it is added.

The Hebrew word for "offering" or "sacrifice" is *korban*. The Hebrew root of *korban* means "near." Etymologically, the word *korban* literally means "that which draws near." In other words, the purpose and function of the temple offerings is to draw the worshipper, the one bringing the offering, closer to God.

This was not the purpose of pagan sacrifice. Pagans had no interest in drawing close to their gods. Their goal in offering sacrifices was to appease the gods and thereby avoid their wrath. They offered beautiful baked breads overlayed with sweetness to please the gods with their beauty. Pagan offerings emphasized aesthetic surface qualities.

By telling us that all offerings must include salt and that no offerings may include honey, the Bible teaches us a powerful lesson about our own worship of God. Our approach to God must never involve masking and covering up who we really are. All our offerings to God must include salt. When we approach God in prayer and worship and attempt to draw ourselves closer to Him, our approach to Him must be an effort to draw out more of our own authentic essence. What we are feeling inside and who we are must honestly emerge and express itself in our worship.

Similarly, all meal offerings were unleavened—simple, humble. The puffed-up external beauty of leavened bread is inappropriate for our korban—our worshipful approach to God.

What was true of the worship in the Tabernacle must be true of our worship as well. Are we masking who we really are with a surface level of sweetness, or are we reaching inward to draw out our authentic selves as we approach God in prayer and worship? Have we allowed spiritual leaven to puff up our egos, or do we come before God with unleavened humility?

Tzav
Leviticus 6:1-8:36

The Lesson of the Sin Offering

MUCH OF TZAV deals with various sacrificial sin offerings. These offerings were to be brought by transgressors to achieve atonement for sin. The different types of sin offerings depend on the type of sin, the manner in which the sin in question was committed, and sometimes by whom it was committed.

At first glance, the entire body of laws relating to animal sacrifices is peculiar. We are certainly aware that most, if not all, pagan sects included some form of sacrifice in their rituals of worship. It is impossible not to notice the similarity between Judaism and the ancient pagans in this regard. In fact, Moses Maimonides (12th century philosopher.) goes so far as to suggest that this similarity is why the Bible commands us to perform sacrifices.

"... and as at that time, the way of life generally accepted and customary in the whole world and the universal service upon which we were brought up consisted in offering various species of living beings in the temples in which images were set up,... His wisdom, may He be exalted, and His gracious

plan, which is manifest in regard to all His creatures, did not require that He give us a law prescribing the rejection, abandonment, and abolition of all these kinds of worship… Therefore, He, may He be exalted, suffered the above-mentioned kinds of worship to remain, but transferred them from created or imaginary and unreal things to His own name, may He be exalted, commanding us to practice them with regard to Him, may he be exalted." (Guide of the Perplexed III:32).

In other words, Maimonides asserts that animal sacrifices were commanded in the Bible due to the fact that the children of Israel at that time were accustomed to worshiping with animal sacrifices and, therefore would be more comfortable worshiping God this way as well.

While the Bible and Paganism share some similarities regarding sacrifices, a number of important distinctions exist between the Pagan sacrificial traditions and the Bible's sacrifices.

One such distinction relates to sin offerings. In Pagan cultures, sacrifices were brought for a variety of purposes. Regarding sin, the idea was that the god or gods were angered by the sin. In order to appease the angered god, an offering must be made. In such cases, the victim was often human. Specifically, the victim would often be the sinner himself. Once the sacrifice has been made, the angry god has been appeased, and all is well. In this system, a person's relationship to the god consists of avoiding angering the god and of offering gifts to keep the god happy. Furthermore, in a situation where the sinner himself was sacrificed, it is obvious that the possibility for repentance was limited. Inasmuch as we may understand the death of the sinner in such cases as punishment for the sin, there is no room for a distinction between penance and punishment.

The Hebrew word for sacrifice is *korban*. A precise etymological translation of this word would be "that which draws close." A person who sins has undermined his relationship to God. The purpose of the offering is to "draw close" to God, to restore the relationship.

As opposed to the Pagan concept of sacrifice, a *korban* is not appeasement for the angered god. We see this most clearly in the fact that a sin offering is only brought when a sin was committed unintentionally. The Bible states this explicitly. On the other hand, if a person sins intentionally, they can not atone by offering a sacrifice.

Think about that. At first glance, this may seem counterintuitive. An intentional sin cannot be atoned for with a sacrificial offering. If the purpose of a sacrifice is to appease the angry God, it would make more sense for offerings to be brought by intentional sinners. Surely, a premeditated sin angers God more than an unintentional mistake.

Pagans understood the importance of penance but lacked a concept of repentance. The basic idea that one who sins must mend their ways and return to a healthy relationship with God was alien to them. The only problem with sinning, for Pagans, is that the gods will be irate. Make the gods happy with a gift or two and they will forget all about the sin.

The Bible sees it differently. An unintentional sin—as opposed to one that is premeditated—results from a lapse in attention to God. One who sins by mistake is not brazenly rebelling against God. Rather, the sinner's careless lack of awareness of God leads to a sin, which in turn causes a spiritual distance between the sinner and God.

Fortunately, the sinner is not forever damned. The relationship with God can be repaired. He needs only to bring a *korban*, to be drawn close to God. He must rebuild his awareness of God so that he will not misstep again in the future.

Our approach to our own religious growth must echo this lesson. We must understand that the optimal response to our own sins is repentance rather than penance. If we sin and then try to pay God off by giving some charity in the hope that it will erase the sin, we are fooling ourselves. God can not be bought. Until the sinful ways have been discarded and replaced with adherence to the will of God, the distance remains.

Sometimes, when we grow distant from those who care about us – be they our parents, God, or anyone else – our inclination is to run even further away to avoid facing the problem. This solution is not a solution and never leads to a harmonious result. Buying back their love with gifts also probably will not suffice. The proper – and more difficult – approach is to "draw close" to those from whom we have grown distant, to approach and mend the relationship by changing our behavior. The result is a stronger, more committed relationship that is freer of guilty feelings. This is repentance. This is how we relate to God, who cares about us, as opposed to a god who does not care and must merely be appeased when angry.

When we sacrifice, we do not give anything up. On the contrary, we only gain. We draw closer and more intimate with God.

Shemini

Leviticus 9:1-11:47

Is Wine Good or Bad?

AS THE PORTION of Shemini opens, we read of the end of the opening ceremonies of the Tabernacle. Much of our portion tells of the events of the eighth day of the consecration. Toward the end of this section, the following law is related:

> *"God spoke to Aaron saying, 'Do not drink wine or any other intoxicant, you and your sons with you when you enter the Tent of Meeting (i.e. the Tabernacle) and you will not die. This is an everlasting statute throughout your generations. And to distinguish between what is sacred and what is mundane, between what is impure and what is pure. And to teach the Children of Israel all of the statutes that God spoke to them through Moses.'" (Leviticus 10:8-11).*

The law here is simple. Priests cannot drink wine or any other intoxicant while serving in or immediately prior to entering the Tabernacle and the Temple in Jerusalem in the future. This is certainly an understandable law. We wouldn't want any drunk priests performing the services.

Based on this law, we might assume that wine has no place in Temple services. This would make wine similar to honey and leaven – as we discussed a few weeks ago – in Leviticus 2:11-13. Of course, this is not the case. Wine is, in fact, a central component of many Temple offerings. Most notably, the daily offerings brought in the morning and afternoon included a wine libation.

While wine is to be offered as a libation in many offerings – public as well as private – no wine is ever drunk as part of any temple service. It is important to note that many of the offerings are meant to be eaten. Many of the animal offerings are eaten. Meal offerings are eaten as well. Wine, while offered, is never consumed.

This leads to a simple question. Is wine good or bad? If it is offered in the Temple, it must be good. If we are forbidden to drink it in the Temple, perhaps it is bad.

In his comments on the daily offering, Rabbi Samson R. Hirsch, the leading rabbi in the German Jewish community in the 19th century, explained the symbolism of the three of ingredients in the daily offering: flour, oil, and wine. Flour represents basic sustenance. Oil represents wealth. Wine represents joy. The purpose of the daily offering is to attribute all of these to God. By bringing this offering daily, we are thanking God for our daily bread (flour), our wealth (oil), and all our joy (wine).

Rabbi Hirsch's comment reminds us of the verse in Psalm 104.

He makes grass grow for the cattle and vegetation for the labor of man, for bringing forth bread from the earth. And wine which gladdens man's heart, oil to make their faces shine, and bread that sustains their hearts. (Psalm 104:14-15).

By offering wine we are stating that we attribute all joy to God. While wine certainly brings joy to people, it does so by altering our senses. If reality as I perceive it is enough to bring me to a joyous state, then I do not require wine. Wine will certainly enhance my joy, but I don't need it. It is only when reality on its own does not bring me joy that wine is needed to produce feelings of joy. The Jewish sages in the Talmud expressed this idea in the following passage:

> *"Rabbi Yehuda ben Beteira states: 'When the Temple was standing, there was no joy without meat. Now that the Temple is no longer standing, there is no joy without wine.'" (Pesachim 109a)*

When the Temple is standing and our relationship to God can be expressed in its ideal form, reality as it is allows for joy. However, in the absence of a Temple, the only hope for joy comes by altering our senses. Reality as it is without a Temple does not allow for joy. It must be enhanced by wine.

Altering our senses with wine in order to feel joyous is not necessarily a bad thing. When we drink wine, we feel happier about whatever we are celebrating. If my favorite sports team just won a championship and I drink, I will feel even happier that they won. If I am drinking four cups of wine on Passover as we retell the story of God's redemption of Israel from Egypt, I will become even more joyous in my praise of God due to the wine.

It makes sense then that while wine enhances feelings of joy, drinking it is forbidden during Temple service. Drinking wine while drawing close to God in the Temple would imply that the experience of closeness to God is insufficient to bring us joy. The lesson here is that there is no greater joy than the experience of drawing close to God in His service. No artificial joy enhancer is necessary.

The great 12th century scholar, Maimonides, in the Guide of

the Perplexed (section III, chs. 45-46), maintains that many of the laws regarding the sacrifices were commanded in order to contradict and counteract the beliefs and practices of ancient pagans. Maimonides offers many examples of this phenomenon in his book. Although he does not mention the prohibition of drinking wine in this context, this law fits nicely into his understanding.

Wine libations were common in virtually all ancient Middle Eastern religious sects. Just as common was the consumption of wine and other intoxicants by the priests performing the services in their temples. Various intoxicating beverages and herbs were a staple of pagan service. Specifically, the sexually oriented pagan festivals invariably included conspicuous wine consumption by the participants.

Among the many mentions of wine offerings in the Torah, one refers to the drinking of a wine libation.

> *He shall say, 'Where is their god, the rock on which they relied for shelter? They ate the fat of their sacrifices, they drank the wine of their libation! Let them arise and help you; let them serve as your shield.' (Deuteronomy 32:37-38).*

At the end of Deuteronomy, Moses poetically refers to God meting out justice on Israel's pagan enemies. This reference to the futility of their false gods mentions two behaviors that are forbidden in the Temple—the eating of fats and the drinking of wine.

The pagans drank wine in the context of religious service and offerings to their gods. The Torah forbids it. Perhaps the lesson is this. Paganism sees the way to transcendence through the altering of the senses in revelry and physical pleasure. Torah sees the way to transcendence through a clear mind drawing close to God.

Tazria

Leviticus 12:1-13:59

Biblical Leprosy and the Power of Words

T HE PORTION OF the Bible, Tazria, deals primarily with the ritual impurity of one who is afflicted with tzaraat, the Biblical skin ailment usually translated as "leprosy." This leprosy is not the same as the condition known today as leprosy. Tzaraat is a physical affliction with a spiritual source. The one afflicted with *tzaraat* is ritually impure and must undergo a unique purification program.

Some restrictions accompany all forms of impurity. Most impurities prohibit one only from entering the Temple. The impurity of a person with *tzaraat* is quite severe. This person is called a *metzora* and the impurity of a *metzora* is the only impurity that requires the one who is impure to leave the city limits and live alone outside the camp. When the *metzora* has been cured and found not to have tzaraat anymore, he then gradually re-enters the life of the community. At the end of this process, he must bring an offering in the Temple.

He [the temple-priest] shall slaughter the [first] lamb in the

place where he slaughters the sin offering and the burnt of-
fering in the sacred place... The priest shall take from the
blood of the guilt offering and the the priest shall put it on
the ridge of the right ear of the person being purified and on
the thumb of his right hand and on the big toe of his right
foot. (Leviticus 14:13-14).

This offering is called a "guilt offering." Many sins, but not all, require the sinner to bring an offering. The standard guilt offerings and sin offerings that would be brought for other sins would never include the placing of blood on the ear, thumb, and toe of the person bringing the offering. This feature is unique to the offering of the *metzora*.

Although this is the only offering that calls for blood to be placed on an ear, thumb, and toe, there is one other instance in the Torah where we see this practice. During the opening cere-monies of the Tabernacle, Aaron, and his sons were initiated as priests. One part of the ceremony was as follows:

Moshe slaughtered [the ram] and took of its blood and put
it on the ridge of Aharon's right ear and upon the thumb of
his right hand and upon the big toe of his right foot. Then
he made the sons of Aharon approach and Moshe put of the
blood upon the ridges of their right ears and upon the thumbs
of their right hands and upon the big toes of their right feet...
(Leviticus 8:23- 24).

Another unique characteristic of the *tzaraat* purification guilt-offering is the following:

The priest shall immerse his right finger in some of the oil
that is in his left palm, and he shall sprinkle some of the oil

with his finger seven times before God. (Leviticus 14:16).

The term "before God" refers to the curtain of the Holy of Holies, the most sacred spot in the Sanctuary. The oil would be sprinkled at the curtain by the temple priest. This feature – like the placing of blood on the ear, thumb, and toe – is peculiar. This is not part of a standard sin offering or of any other offering brought by an individual. The blood of a standard sin offering is sprinkled on the altar, not the curtain of the Holy of Holies.

The altar was located in the courtyard of the Temple. The Holy of Holies is the Temple's innermost chamber. Aside from this offering of the *metzora*, there are only two other situations that call for sprinkling on this curtain. One is when an offering was brought to atone for a sin committed by the High Priest himself. The other situation is an offering brought to atone for a sin committed by the entire community of Israel. (see Leviticus 4:6,17) These two situations are similar. The High Priest is a public figure. He represents the entire nation in his service before God. His own sins can never be considered private.

All of this only serves to underscore our questions. Why is the guilt offering of the *metzora* singled out in this way, requiring features otherwise reserved for sins committed by the entire community or by the High Priest? Why does the purification process of the *metzora* share a feature with the inauguration ceremony of Aaron and his sons? Why is *tzaraat* impurity so severe that it requires removal from the camp of Israel?

According to Jewish tradition, *tzaraat* afflicts a person directly from the sin of tale-bearing, gossiping, and speaking ill of others. This tradition originates with the story of Miriam, Moses' and Aaron's sister. In Numbers 12 we read of her being afflicted with leprosy as a response from God for speaking ill of Moses.

By banishing the *metzora* from the camp, the Torah teaches us that the sin of speaking ill of others is so *impure* that the *metzora* must be exiled from the community. The punishment fits the crime. Speaking ill of others is malicious and anti-social. Often, the goal of the talebearer is the exclusion or "canceling" of the person about whom the tale is being told. The result of this punishment is that the talebearer, rather than the subject of the tale, is deemed unfit for social interaction and must leave the camp.

As long as the blemish of *tzaraat* is present, the *metzora* cannot re-enter the community. Theoretically, if the talebearer afflicted with *tzaraat* were never to repent and thus never to heal, the excommunication would be permanent. Effectively, such a person would cease to be a member of the community of Israel.

As mentioned above, no other form of impurity requires complete removal from the community. The process of purification and repentance is unique because we are not dealing with a normal sin or usual impurity. A recovering *metzora* is not merely becoming purified. He is recovering his status as a member of the community of Israel.

In their inauguration to become Temple priests, Aaron and his sons underwent an elevation in status from normal Israelites to priests. This new status gave them access to places non-priests can not go. It entitled them to special gifts and privileges. It also brought restrictions that do not apply to the rest of the community. Their status was elevated. Let me put it this way, prior to the inauguration ceremony, Aaron and his sons were regular members of the nation of Israel. After the ceremony, they had a unique and higher spiritual status.

Similarly, the *metzora* must undergo a change in status from a *metzora* who must be removed from the camp, to being restored to the regular status of a full member of the community of Israel. The *metzora's* exile sends the message that he is no longer a full member of the people of Israel. Upon re-entry to the community, he must dedicate himself to a more elevated life than he led before. Just as the sons of Aaron rose in status from regular Israelite to priest, the recovered *metzora* rises in status from excommunicated *metzora* to full member of the community. The priests' initiation ceremony and the metzora's purification accomplish the same goal. The elevation of status from a lower level to a higher one. This is expressed by the shared procedure involving the ear, thumb, and toe. (a full treatment of the meaning of this particular procedure is beyond the scope of this article.)

Rabbi Yisrael Meir Kagan (1838-1933), a leading rabbi in prewar Europe, explained the requirement of a *metzora* to sprinkle oil on the curtain of the Holy of Holies, similar to the atonement for a sin of the High Priest or of the entire community. The impact of a sin by the High Priest is greater than the sin of an ordinary citizen. This makes sense. When spiritual leaders of great influence sin, the impact is far greater than the sins committed by the rest of us. In a sense, there is no private sin when it comes to people of great spiritual influence. In this way, the sin of a High Priest is similar to a sin by the entire community. It is a public matter. Both such sins speak to the deterioration of communal morality and ethics.

Rabbi Kagan goes on to explain that this is why a sin by a private citizen is atoned for on the altar in the courtyard of the Temple. Still, a sin by the High Priest – or the entire community - must be atoned for in the most sacred of places, the curtain of the Holy of Holies. The message Rabbi Kagan explains is that speaking ill of other people is not a private sin. Stories are repeated and shared. Slander and gossip destroy relationships and communities.

The Torah teaches us a powerful lesson by linking the purification process of the metzora to the inauguration of the priests, the sins of the High Priest, and the sine of the community. The sin of talebearing—of spreading negative information with the intent of damaging others—is not a private matter. God granted human beings, and only human beings, the power of speech. We must be careful to use this unique ability only for the good.

Death and life are in the power of the tongue, and those who love it will eat its fruit. (Proverbs 18:21).

Metzora

Leviticus 14:1–15:33

Leprosy: A Gift from God

M OST OF THE Bible Portion, Metzora is devoted to the plague of *tzara'at*, usually translated as leprosy. The Bible relates detailed descriptions of different types of leprous spots, discolorations, and several other skin ailments. According to the instructions in these chapters, these ailments are to be dealt with not by a dermatologist but by a priest, from the family of Aaron. The priest would declare these symptoms impure or pure, and they would be dealt with accordingly.

The text appears to be discussing problems of a medical nature until chapter 13, verse 47, when leprous spots on clothing and later (14:34) on the walls of a house are introduced.

> *"God spoke to Moses saying: When you will come to the land of Canaan, which I give to you as a possession, I will put a plague of leprosy in a house of the land of your possession." (Leviticus 14:33-34).*

Leprosy on a house or on one's clothing is certainly not within the usual range of medical problems. Furthermore, the above verse introduces the topic of "leprosy in a house" with the phrase, "When you will come into the land of Canaan," which clearly implies that there is some connection between the land of Israel (or Canaan) and the appearance of leprous spots on homes. It is important to note that most laws in the Bible are not introduced with the phrase "When you come to the land…"

What's more, as if to emphasize the connection between the land of Israel and leprosy on homes, the verse also ends by saying that this will occur "in a house of the land of your possession." A rule of thumb when reading the Bible is that any apparently needless repetition is the Bible's way of emphasizing a point. In this case, it seems, that what is being emphasized is the connection between the land and this strange disease afflicting the walls of homes.

The great commentator and Rabbinic leader Rabbi Moses Nachmanides (13th century Spain) explains that since leprosy on houses and clothing is obviously "not in the natural order of things," it is clearly a sign from God. He goes on to say that this divine leprosy is a sign that the afflicted person or the owner of the possessions has sinned and that "God has turned aside from him." He goes on to write that such a sign from God that one has sinned will only happen in the land "wherein the Glorious Name dwells." Why should such a sign be restricted to the Land of Israel?

It seems that in Nachmanides view since these leprous conditions are signs from God that a person has sinned, leprosy is – like prophecy – a revelation from God. Simply stated, when a person is afflicted with this "leprosy," it ought to be understood as a communication directly from God to the afflicted person.

This brings us back to our original question: Why only in the land of Israel?

There are many ways that the land of Israel is special. Aside from being the place that God chose to give to His people, Israel, this land possesses a sanctity and spirituality that does not exist elsewhere. This special status finds expression in many ways. One of the ways we see the special spirituality of the land of Israel is through the fact that many of the commandments in the Bible can be fulfilled only in the land of Israel. For example, all the agricultural laws, such as the tithing laws, the sabbatical, and jubilee years, are only practiced in the land. More broadly, the many national commandments related to proper governance of the nation of Israel can be fulfilled only in the land of Israel.

Due to the many commandments that are only applicable in the Land of Israel, one who lives in the Land of Israel has the ability to observe more of the Bible – God's expressed will. Greater observance of God's will naturally produces a stronger and more intimate relationship to God. For this reason, Jewish tradition teaches that full prophecy – the direct and clear communication from God to human beings – requires a closeness that can only be achieved in the Land of Israel.

"Until the Land of Israel was chosen, all lands were suitable for the word [of prophecy]. Since the Land of Israel was chosen, all other lands are unsuitable. When Jerusalem was destroyed the word [of prophecy] was banished from the Land of Israel." - Midrash Tanchuma Bo 5

To sum up the theological logic of this important idea, prophecy within the people of Israel can only exist in the land of Israel because the conditions of holiness required to experience prophecy only exist in the Holy Land, where the Bible can be fully fulfilled. The destruction of the Temple in Jerusalem greatly diminished the intimacy of the relationship between God and Israel. The service of God in the Temple could no longer take place. His people could now fulfil less of God's will. As a result, the intimacy of Israel's relationship with God suffered. This diminished relationship does not allow for direct communication in the form of prophecy.

Leprosy, then, can be seen as a physical form of prophecy. A person has sinned, and now, by afflicting the person or his possessions with leprosy, God is communicating that this sin has caused His relationship with that person to suffer.

When people struggle with faith in God they often say, "If only God would give me a sign…" But receiving a sign from God is no small matter. To receive a sign from God, one must be on a spiritual level to merit such a sign. Imagine someone who says, "I'd believe in God if only He would talk to me directly." Obviously, that is an unreasonable demand. It is unreasonable because prophecy – God speaking directly to people – is bestowed on a person of elevated spiritual stature who has worked to achieve a powerfully deep and devoted relationship to God. Hearing God's "voice" or receiving signs and messages from God requires spiritual refinement to the point that one can receive such messages and signs.

Rabbi Ovadiah Seforno, (Italy 1475-1550), in his commentary to this Bible portion (Leviticus 3:47), writes that leprosy of the kind discussed here only affected those members of the community who were on a high enough spiritual level to "merit" it. It is remarkable that what appears to be a cursed illness that punishes sinners would be reserved for those who are on a high spiritual level. It does not seem fair that one who is on a lower spiritual level does not have to worry about this punishment, while those who have a closer relationship with God do.

There is a powerful moral lesson in all of this. Any clearly communicated message from God is a blessing. A message from God that alerts one to a crisis in one's relationship with God is invaluable. Imagine having a clear and obvious barometer informing you when your relationship with God is healthy and needs a little work.

May we all merit to be worthy of such punishments from God.

Achrei Mot

Leviticus 16:1–18:30

The Two Goats

THE BIBLICAL DESCRIPTION of every festival includes instructions for sacrificial offerings in the temple. Yom Kippur, the Day of Atonement, is no different. However, there is one temple ritual that is unique to Yom Kippur and highly unusual. Leviticus 16 describes the Yom Kippur temple rituals performed by Aaron, the high priest, and all subsequent high priests after him.

> *Then he is to take the two goats and present them before the Lord at the entrance to the tent of meeting. He is to cast lots for the two goats—one lot for the Lord and the other for the scapegoat. Aaron shall bring the goat whose lot falls to the Lord and sacrifice it for a sin offering. But the goat chosen by lot as the scapegoat shall be presented alive before the Lord to be used for making atonement by sending it into the wilderness as a scapegoat.... "When Aaron has finished making atonement for the Most Holy Place, the tent of meeting and the altar, he shall bring forward the live goat. He is to lay both hands on the head of the live goat and confess over it all the wickedness and rebellion of the Israelites—all their*

sins—and put them on the goat's head. He shall send the goat
away into the wilderness in the care of someone appointed
for the task. The goat will carry on itself all their sins to a
remote place, and the man shall release it in the wilderness.
Leviticus 16:7-10, 20-22).

To sum up, the high priest must take two goats and place them at the entrance of the temple. He then casts lots to decide which one will be offered for the Lord on the altar in the Temple and which one will be the scapegoat. After offering the first goat to the Lord on the altar, the high priest would place his hands on the second goat, confess all the sins of Israel over the goat, and send it into the wilderness – literally in Hebrew, the desert - with someone appointed for the task.

Ancient Jewish tradition adds a number of important details of this procedure. The two goats chosen for this ritual were to be as identical as possible. They were the same age and size and needed to be as close to each other in appearance as could be found. When the second goat was let out into the wilderness, it was brought to a cliff, where it was thrown to its death. As for the choosing of the person who was appointed for the task of leading the scapegoat out into the desert, there is a fascinating tradition based on puzzling words in the original Hebrew here in Leviticus.

Verse 21 quoted above, states that the High Priest would send the goat away into the wilderness in the care of someone appointed for the task – *ish iti* in Hebrew. *Ish* is Hebrew for "man." *Iti* is difficult to translate, but it certainly does not mean "appointed for the task." In fact, in no place in the Bible does this word root mean "appointed" or anything similar. The literal translation of *iti* is "timely" or "momentary." In other words, the literal translation of the end of verse 21 is, "Send the goat away into the wilderness in the care of a timely man." Translators solve this strange word choice by interpreting it to mean a man who was chosen or appointed for this specific moment. Still, the choice of words in the Bible is unusual and worthy of our attention.

Based on this word, Jewish tradition teaches that the person chosen for this task was selected based on the knowledge that he would not live out the year. Whether this was known prophetically or medically is not mentioned in the tradition.

Let us now put all the details together. Two identical goats stand at the entrance to the temple. One will enter the Temple as an offering to the Lord. The other goat will carry the burden of all Israel's sins into the desert, where nothing grows, by a man who has no future. There, it will die a pointless death and be wasted.

The ritual of the two goats of Yom Kippur is a metaphor for the life of every one of us, every single day. Think of the two goats as two options for the same life. This is the reason why they were identical in every way. Like those goats, every day, we stand at the entrance to the temple – the place of service to God. The choice is before us. We can enter the temple and dedicate our lives to the Lord, or we can choose the path of sin, leading to barrenness, destruction, and waste. And like the momentary man, sin has no plan for the future. Every person witnessing this event each year in the temple was reminded of the choices that lie before us every day. Are we for the Lord, or are we headed to the wilderness?

There is another Biblical symbol that is alluded to by these two goats. Consider the story of Isaac and Ishmael. Both were sons of Abraham. Both began their lives in the same home. In Abraham's well-known story of the binding of Isaac, Isaac was offered as a sacrifice to God. Ishmael, on the other hand, was banished to the desert because of his sinful behavior. (Genesis 21:9) While the Bible describes what Ishmael did vaguely as "mocking", the

Hebrew word in this verse for mocking is the same word used to describe the immoral and idolatrous behavior of the children of Israel at the sin of the Golden Calf.

Afterward, they sat down to eat and drink and got up to indulge in revelry [Heb.- le'tzachek]. – (Exodus 32:6) – The Golden Calf.

But Sarah saw that the son whom Hagar the Egyptian had borne to Abraham was mocking [Heb. - me'tzachek Genesis 21:9) The banishing of Ishmael.

In other words, despite the ambiguous English translation, the Bible describes Ishmael as involved in overtly sinful behavior.

Ishmael, who was circumcised and was brought into the covenant of Abraham, chose a life of sin rather than a life of dedicated service to God. On the other hand, Isaac willingly offered his life to God.

This is the message the Day of Atonement. God has put us in this world for a purpose. We can choose to embrace that purpose and live a life of dedication to Him and His kingdom, or we can choose the path that leads to the wilderness; a place of destruction where nothing grows, and nothing lives.

Kedoshim

Leviticus 19:1–20:27

Respect for Elders as a Tenet of Our Faith

IN THE PORTION of Kedoshim, within a lengthy list of commandments, we read:

In the presence of the elderly, you shall rise, and you shall respect an elder; you shall fear your God, I am Hashem. (Leviticus 19:32).

This commandment – respect for the elderly – is easily understandable. Most familiar to us as the fifth of the Ten Commandments, respect for parents and grandparents is the cornerstone of strong family relationships, which in turn leads to a healthier society as a whole. What is unusual about the commandment, as stated here in Leviticus 19, is the context in which it appears in the Bible.

Anyone who has ever seen the inside of a Bible scroll is aware that the text appears in sections with spaces separating the sections. These sections do not correspond to the chapter numbers that we are used to, which were developed by Christian scholars centuries later. It is these section breaks, the original meaning of the term *parasha* or portion refers to these sections.

This verse is the last of a ten-verse section that mostly deals with forbidden pagan practices. Based on this context, those laws in this section that don't seem to be obviously referring to paganism, such as the prohibition against eating blood and allowing one's daughter to become a prostitute, are properly understood as responses to behaviors that were associated with idolatrous practices common in the Ancient Near East. Even the opening law of the section, the agricultural rules of *orlah*, the prohibition against eating fruit of the first three years of a tree's growth is understood by some to have its root in the negation of certain pagan beliefs and customs. (see Nachmanides here, and Maimonides Guide for the Perplexed III:37)

This leads to an obvious question regarding the verse we are discussing. What possible connection is there between honoring the elderly and the importance of avoiding the immorality of pagan beliefs and ways? Why specifically is this commandment linked to the general injunction to fear God, as the verse concludes, "You shall fear God, I am the Lord"?

In the preface to his classic work on paganism, The Golden Bough, Sir James Frazer writes that the fear of death and of the dead is "on the whole, probably the most powerful force in the making of primitive religion."

Ancient paganism was obsessed with death because pagans focused their entire system of faith on the forces that govern the natural world. They feared death so strongly because they believed that they – like everything else in the natural world – were finite and mortal.

Everything in the natural physical world follows the same trajectory of life and growth. Every living thing is born or comes to life. In the first third to a quarter of its lifespan, it grows to its peak of size, beauty, and strength. From this peak, a gradual decline in strength and vitality begins until finally dying. This is the way of all living things, including plants, animals, and humans.

The exception to this rule is *the human soul*. A human being does not peak emotionally, intellectually, and spiritually at the same time as the body reaches its peak of health and strength. The soul of man continues to develop and grow long after the body has begun its decline towards death. In fact, the soul, if left unimpeded by the interference of the deterioration of the body, continues to grow stronger throughout life. The body, on the other hand, no matter how good the conditioning or nutritional program, inevitably deteriorates, if only gradually.

Seen this way, the soul is – in effect – immune from the rules of the rest of physical, organic life. The human soul does not follow the rules of the natural trajectory of life, growth, decline, and death.

For an ideology that sees physical nature as the only mode of existence – in a society that values the body as the primary focus of the human experience – a person whose body is at its peak of strength and beauty will be revered. If, on the other hand, the *spiritual* is valued as the highest purpose and definition of vitality, honor will be given to those whose souls are more fully developed. By commanding us to honor the elderly, the Bible teaches us that the essence of the human being is spiritual. Honoring our elders is a statement that we value the soul over the body.

The Bible uses an unusual verb in the commandment to respect the elderly. The Hebrew words are *vehadarta pnei zaken*. *Vehadarta* does not really mean "you shall respect." In fact, *vehadarta* is a second-person verb conjugation of the word *hadar*, which usually translates as "beauty." For example:

And you shall take for yourselves on the first day the fruit of beautiful [*hadar*] trees, branches of palm trees, the boughs of leafy trees, and willows of the brook; and you shall rejoice before the Lord your God for seven days. – Leviticus 23:40

Many flowers will grow in it, and it will be filled with joy and singing. The greatness of Lebanon will be given to it, and the beauty [*hadar*] of Carmel and Sharon. They will see the shining greatness of the Lord, the wonderful power of our God. (Isaiah 35:2).

In addition, the verse doesn't say, "Respect an elder." The literal Hebrew says, "Respect the face of an elder."

Putting these two notable word choices together, the exact translation of the commandment is probably closer to "you shall find beauty in the face of an elder." This is certainly an etymologically accurate rendering of the syntax.

How fitting.

There is a powerful natural inclination to be impressed by youthful beauty. Youthful strength and beauty are very physically appealing. The Bible is telling us that this mistaken view sees only the natural physical side of things. The essence of humanity is the soul. The spiritual side of humanity is beyond the natural experience of the body. We are to look beyond the natural and physical. We are called upon to see the true human beauty. If we see things correctly, the result will be that we will, in the words of the verse, "find beauty in the face of an elder."

The verse ends with the injunction to fear God. The connection is clear. When we say that man was created in the image of God, we mean the soul, not the body. Proper respect for the elderly constitutes rejection of a physically-centered existence and acceptance of a spiritual reality.

May we all strengthen our connections to the elderly, our greatest sources of wisdom and spiritual guidance.

Emor

Mourning Laws: Bible vs. Paganism

T HE OPENING VERSES of this week's parashah deal with some of the laws of the purity of the *kohanim*, the temple priests from the family of Aaron. Specifically, the text outlines restrictions on mourning practices. Among these restrictions, we read:

"They shall not make baldness on their heads and the corners of their beards they shall not shave, and they shall not make gashes in their flesh." (Leviticus 21:5).

(Although the text relates these prohibitions only to the priestly family, the rabbinic tradition extended these rules to the entire community of Israel (see Babylonian Talmud Makot 20a).)

To sum up, in this verse, the Bible prohibits three mourning practices.

No ripping out of hair to "make baldness on their heads"
No shaving the corners of their beards
No gashes in the flesh

To appreciate the meaning behind these prohibitions, we

must first understand the intent of the practices that are being forbidden. To the modern reader, the gashing of flesh and tearing out of hair appear to be expressions of grief. We imagine a mourner who is pained at the loss of a loved one. Overcome by grief, the mourner lashes out at himself by tearing the hair out of his head and gashing his flesh.

Although incorrect, this understanding of these practices, that they were spontaneous displays of uncontrollable grief, still only works for the first and third prohibitions. But what about shaving? Why would a grief-stricken mourner shave his beard?

Sir James Frazer, best known for his classic work on ancient pagan beliefs and practices, *The Golden Bough*, discusses ancient pagan mourning practices in another work, *Folk-Lore in the Old Testament* (Macmillan 1923). Frazer devotes twenty pages of this book to the ritual cutting of the hair and gashing the flesh by mourners. He details the customs of literally dozens of pagan tribes from all parts of the world who engaged in similar practices. The customs of these many varied tribes were more alike than different. They were alike in a number of prominent ways.

First, the gashing of the skin – the most common mourning ritual among ancient religions – was not a spontaneous act by delirious grief-stricken mourners. In fact, it was quite intentional, ordered, and followed set ritual procedures and norms. Second, the cutting of hair was not, by and large, the tearing of hair from the head as a spontaneous act of grief. Rather, this shaving of hair from the head - "making baldness" – was done with scissors or a blade. Like the gashing of the skin, this haircutting was ritualized and ordered. Third, by and large, beard shaving was done to collect the shaven hair for ritual use at the funeral.

Frazer shows quite conclusively that the cut and shaved hair, along with the blood from the skin gashes, were intended as offerings to the deceased. Often the hair would actually be thrown into the grave with the body. Expression of grief was decidedly not the purpose of these rituals. Rather, they were meant to appease and, in some cases, worship the dead.

Frazer concludes the chapter – "Cuttings for the Dead" pp. 377-397 – with this explanation:

> *"The widespread practices of cutting the bodies and shearing the hair of the living after a death were originally designed to gratify or benefit in some way the spirit of the departed; and accordingly, wherever such customs have prevailed, they may be taken as evidence that the people who observed them believed in the survival of the human soul after death and desired to maintain friendly relations with it. In other words, the observance of these usages implies a propitiation or worship of the dead." (Folklore in the Old Testament; Chap. IV, pp. 397)*

We see from the above that the central meaning of this prohibition is not so much to forbid harming our bodies in the course of grieving, although this too is certainly prohibited. The primary focus of these laws is to combat the prevalent pagan ideals of reverence for and worship of the dead.

It is interesting to note that one of the key Jewish observances in the early stages of mourning is a prohibition on shaving and cutting one's hair, which is the exact opposite of the pagan custom.

In both last week's column as well as this one, I have highlighted the way that many of the Bible's commandments were intended to counteract the pagan impulse to glorify death. As I quoted from Frazer's *The Golden Bough* last week, "fear of death and of the dead is on the whole, probably the most powerful force in the making of primitive religion."

In light of this, it is important to note that the Temple priests, the *kohanim*, those who were at the center of the life of worship of God, were commanded to avoid contact with the dead. As we read in the opening verse of this Bible portion, a few verses before the one we are studying.

The Lord said to Moses, "Speak to the priests, the sons of Aaron, and say to them: 'A priest must not make himself ceremonially unclean for any of his people who die." (Leviticus 21:1).

Contact with a dead human body conveys a severe level of ritual impurity. There is nothing objectively wrong with becoming ritually impure. Those who do the sacred work of proper care for and burial of the deceased become impure in this way, even though they are performing a sacred duty. Impurity is not about sin. It is about being exposed to that which darkens our spiritual lives.

In pagan worship, death was front and center. Human sacrifice and worship of dead ancestors were widespread across the ancient religions of the globe. It could be argued that the priests and spiritual leaders of these pagan religions were more involved with death than almost anyone else in society. In contrast, the Bible demands that those whose role it is to lead us in the worship of God must be as far as possible from death. They must not have death and mortality on the minds. The reason is simple. Faith in the God of Israel focuses on life in this world and the next.

Reverence for death and the dead is a primary component of Pagan belief systems. The Bible opposes this. The Bible's way is the way of life.

"Life and death have I placed before you, blessing and curse; you shall choose life in order that you live, you and your descendants." (Deuteronomy 30:19).

Behar

Leviticus 25:1-26:2

The Lessons of
the Jubilee Year

*You shall sanctify the year of the fiftieth year and proclaim
freedom in the land for all of its inhabitants; it shall be for
you a jubilee, and each man shall return to his ancestral land,
and each man shall return to his family." (Leviticus 25:8,10).*

THE BIBLE PORTION, Behar, includes the rules for the Jubilee
Year. As we read in this passage, the Torah commands that
two laws take effect every fifty years. All Israelite slaves would be
freed, and all lands would be redistributed back to their original
tribal owners. In other words, anyone who had sold his land since
the last jubilee regains full ownership of the land at the jubilee.

At first glance, this seems unfair to the purchaser of the land.
Why should this person have to surrender land that was legally
purchased? To solve this problem, the Bible lays out a system for
purchasing land according to the years of the jubilee.

*"According to the number of years after the jubilee shall you
purchase land from your neighbor; according to the number*

of produce years he shall sell it to you. Based on the abun-
dance of years, you shall increase its purchase price, and based
on the lack of years, you shall decrease its purchase price since
it is the number of produce seasons that he is selling to you."
(Leviticus 25:15-16).

When land is sold, the price is calculated based on the amount of time that the land will be owned by the purchaser – until the next jubilee. Essentially, all land purchases in Israel are to be leases rather than actual purchases. According to the Jewish sages, even if one were to attempt to sell land permanently, the transaction would be invalid. The land is forever owned by the family to whom it was allotted after the original conquest of the land. However, even if these guidelines were not followed, the land would still return to its original owner. No financial recompense would be made to the purchaser of the land. The original owner gets the land back free of charge.

At first glance, the redistribution of land to its original owners appears to be consistent with socialist policies of redistribution of wealth familiar to us in modern times. Certain individuals' ability to build empires by continually acquiring more land is obviously curtailed. At the same time, the impoverished who have lost everything get a fresh start.

A closer look reveals that the jubilee system differs from modern redistributionist policies in several important ways.

One of the main complaints against policies that call for a redistribution of wealth is that it is not fair. It is hard to make a living to then be forced to support someone who is too lazy to work. Indeed, it is unfair.

On the other hand, proponents of redistribution argue that without redistribution, there is scarcely a chance for the poorer elements in society to get on their feet. Once they have no significant assets and are at the mercy of the wealthy, there is no way out.

The jubilee system solves both of these concerns. The 20th-century French economist Bertrand de Jouvenel, in his *Ethics of Redistribution*, points out that the Biblical jubilee system does not advocate a redistribution of product or profit. Rather, it is a redistribution of resources. As such, the injustice of taking profit from those who worked for it and giving to those who did not is absent. On the other hand, by redistributing valuable resources – land – every citizen is given a fair chance to make the most of his assets and begin to build independent wealth.

Let's consider a person who would sell his ancestral family plot of land in an agrarian society such as Biblical Israel. He probably experienced some kind of financial hardship that led him to sell this land that was passed down to him through the generations, all the way back to the original distribution of the land in the days of Joshua. Upon the arrival of the jubilee year, he regains ownership and control of his land. He gets a fresh start.

Free of charge, he is now able to work the land, mortgage it, and sell it until the following jubilee year; he can use this valuable asset to generate wealth.

The Bible believes in fairness and freedom. In admittedly very simplistic terms, modern socialism advocates fairness at the expense of freedom. Unbridled free market capitalism advocates freedom at the expense of fairness. The Bible's economic system treats all citizens as equals while rewarding those who worked hard with the full fruits of their labor.

But there is more to these laws than economics. Allow me to explain.

Throughout centuries of persecution, one of the most common restrictions placed on Jews in the lands of exile was the prohibition from owning land. Even today, there are Arab countries that forbid Jews from owning land. To own land is to be a full citizen—to be free. Land ownership is critical to national identification. To be forbidden from owning land is to be excluded—to be forever a foreigner.

The rules of land ownership and the jubilee teach us a profound lesson. All Jews are landowners forever. There are no serfs. In fact, each and every Jew alive today has a plot of land that actually belongs to him by patrimonial birthright. If the laws of jubilee were in effect today, the land owned by my family would return to us. It has always been ours.

Throughout the centuries of our exile, the same Jews who were being denied rights of land ownership in the lands of the dispersion were, at the same time, owners of land in Israel forever.

Seen this way, the Jewish people's connection to the land of Israel is not only a religious or historical connection. Wherever we are, it remains our birthright and our literal home.

Bechukotai

Leviticus 26:3-27:34

The Reverse Order
of the Covenants

*I will remember my covenant with Jacob, my covenant with
Isaac, and my covenant with Abraham, and I will remember
the land (Leviticus 26:42).*

I N A LENGTHY passage describing the punishments that will
befall the people of Israel, God reminds us that despite all
the suffering and exile, He will always adhere to the covenant
He made with the patriarchs Abraham, Isaac, and Jacob. The
most glaring question that comes to mind when encountering
this verse is: Why is Jacob, the last of the patriarchs, listed first?

To appreciate the significance of this anomaly, let's first look
at the verse in context.

'But if they confess their iniquity and the iniquity of their
fathers, with their unfaithfulness in which they were unfaithful
to Me, and that they also have walked contrary to Me, and that
I also have walked contrary to them and have brought them
into the land of their enemies; if their uncircumcised hearts are
humbled, and they accept their guilt— then I will remember My

covenant with Jacob and My covenant with Isaac and My covenant with Abraham I will remember, and I will remember the land. The land also shall be left empty by them and will enjoy its sabbaths while it lies desolate without them; they will accept their guilt, because they despised My judgments and because their soul abhorred My statutes. (Leviticus 26:40-43).

At this point in the narrative of the future punishments of Israel, they have been banished into exile. And from the verse that follows ours we see that they remain there at this point. With this in mind, we can understand the unusual reverse order of the patriarchs.

Jacob is the only one of the three patriarchs who went into exile after being born in the land of Israel. He is the only one who suffered in exile, as he did while living under his uncle Laban. And when Jacob went into exile a second time, this time to Egypt, God made a promise to him that has been the hope of the Jewish people throughout our history.

"I will go down to Egypt with you, and I will surely bring you back again." Genesis 46:4).

Jacob is the first patriarch mentioned here because Jacob is the patriarch who represents the Jewish experience of exile. The "covenant with Jacob" is God's promise to always be with us in exile and to come out of exile with us.

Isaac was born in the land but never left it. And this was not simply due to good fortune. On two occasions, Isaac should have left the land but did not. The first is when Abraham sent his servant, rather than Isaac himself, to the land of Haran to find a wife for Isaac. The reason Isaac was not sent?

But Abraham said to him, "Beware that you do not take my son back there. The Lord God of heaven, who took me from my father's house and from the land of my family, and who spoke to me and swore to me, saying, 'To your descendants, I give this land,' He will send His angel before you, and you shall take a wife for my son from there. And if the woman is unwilling to follow you, you will be released from this oath; only do not take my son back there." (Genesis 24:6-8).

Later, when there was a famine in the land, Isaac started out for Egypt, as his father had done under similar circumstances. This time, it was God who prevented Isaac from leaving the land. (see Genesis 26:2-3). Clearly, it was a necessary part of God's plan for Isaac to remain in the land and to never leave. Isaac then embarked on a mission to reclaim disputed territories that were part of the covenant from the Philistines who had taken them. While it is beyond the scope of this current teaching, it is safe to say that the "covenant of Isaac" is all about asserting ownership of the land.

Abraham was born outside the land and left it after entering. But unlike Jacob, he never suffered and was never subservient in exile. Abraham's mission was a universal one. His name was changed to Abraham because "A father of a multitude of nations I have placed you." His calling was to bring blessing to all the families of the earth. In his personality as well, we see Abraham's universalism. He was opposed to banishing Ishmael. He tried to make peace with the Philistines. He prayed for Sodom and Gomorrah.

To sum up, the three patriarchs represent three different aspects of Israel's covenantal mission. Abraham represents the universal mission to bring knowledge of God to all humanity. Isaac represents the more particularistic covenant of land. Jacob represents the Jewish experience throughout history, going into exile, suffering, and ultimately returning to the land.

Now we can understand why the patriarchs are listed in reverse order in Leviticus 26. This verse speaks to a situation in which the people of Israel are mired in exile. The reverse order of the patriarchs describes the process of emerging from that exile to the full fulfillment of their covenantal purpose and mission.

First, God will remember His covenant with Jacob. In other words, He will protect them and redeem them from exile. Then, He will restore the covenant of Isaac, bringing His people back to their land in full independence and sovereignty. Finally, God will enable Israel to fulfill their highest calling in fulfillment of the covenant with Abraham, to be the source of blessing for all the families of the earth.

Numbers

Bamidbar

Numbers 1:1–4:20

Enlistment in God's Army

THE BIBLE PORTION of Bamidbar describes the first census of the children of Israel. One of God's instructions to Moses was that he should not count the tribe of Levi among the other tribes. They were to be counted separately. Later, after the census of everyone else was complete, God commanded Moses to count the Levites. (3:15) But just before God's command to count the Levites, God told Moses the following:

"God spoke to Moses saying, 'Behold! I have taken the Levites from among the Children of Israel, in place of every firstborn, the first issue of every womb among the Children of Israel, and the Levites shall be Mine. For every firstborn is Mine: On the day I struck down every firstborn in Egypt, I sanctified every firstborn in Israel for Myself, from man to beast; they shall be Mine – I am the Lord." Numbers 3:11-13).

Later in the chapter, after the Levites were counted, Moses was commanded to count the firstborns of the other tribes and to exchange them for the Levites. In other words, each firstborn of the other tribes would have his priestly status transferred to a Levite. Because there were more firstborns than Levites, any remaining firstborns that had not been matched up with a Levite were to be redeemed for five silver shekels. (3:40-51) This redemption for five silver shekels is the rule to this day. Firstborn males of any non-Levite family are redeemed from a *kohen* – a priest from the descendants of Aaron - for five silver shekels.

According to this passage, God chose the firstborns of Israel on the night that He "struck down every firstborn in the land of Egypt." He later chose the Levites to replace the firstborns of Israel. The Levites were thus chosen to perform the various services in the Tabernacle and to take care of the Tabernacle during travel. Rashi (11th century France), the greatest of all Jewish commentators, explains:

> *For service was done by the firstborns, but when they sinned at the Golden Calf they were disqualified, and the Levites who did not worship idolatry were chosen in their place. (Rashi, Numbers 3:12).*

Let's sum up what we have seen from these verses with the help of Rashi. The firstborn males were originally chosen for the priestly role in Israel. They were selected on the night of the plague of the firstborns when all Egyptian firstborns were killed. Later, due to their role in the sin of the Golden Calf, they lost this status. They were replaced by the Levites, who did not sin.

To fully understand this complex issue, let's examine the two events mentioned above: the plague of the firstborns and the sin of the golden Calf.

The Plague of the Firstborns

Let us review the events of that great and historic night. The night before the Exodus from Egypt, at exactly midnight, God killed every firstborn male in Egypt except for certain firstborns of Israel. Those Israelites who heeded the command of God were spared. If the Passover offering was slaughtered and the blood was placed on the doorposts and doorframe of the house, the firstborn of that house was safe. This Paschal lamb was the very first sacrificial offering brought by the Jewish people in their history as a nation. While all the children of Israel ate from the offering, the Paschal sacrifice had much greater significance for the firstborns. For them, the proper execution of God's orders was a matter of life and death.

The truth is that every sacrifice is a matter of life and death, at least symbolically. The meaning behind all animal sacrifices is that the one bringing the sacrifice is meant to identify with the animal and realize that ideally, it is he, rather than the animal, that deserves to be offered up to God. The illustrative paradigm of this idea is the binding of Isaac by Abraham in Genesis 22. Abraham was willing to sacrifice his son, who was then replaced by a ram. When the Paschal sacrifice was made in Egypt, this idea that the offering serves as a replacement and redemption for the life of the person was no doubt felt most profoundly by the firstborns of Israel. After all, for them, it really was a question of either the death of a lamb or their own deaths.

Considering this backdrop, it was only natural that it was the firstborn of each family who actually carried out the slaughtering of the animal and the smearing of the doorposts with blood. Rashi alluded to this when he stated that the service had previously been done by the firstborns. Since there were no other sacrifices offered by Israel prior to the sin of the Golden Calf, what else could Rashi have meant when he wrote that prior to that sin, service was performed by the firstborns of Israel? By decreeing death for the firstborns of any family that failed to perform the Paschal offering, God created a situation wherein the firstborns of Israel became the primary focus and performers of the Children of Israel's first sacrificial service to God, the Paschal offering. Through this process, the firstborns were chosen for Temple service.

After Moses descended Mount Sinai, saw the Golden Calf, and broke the tablets, he set to work rectifying the situation. Moses' first task was to see who was still loyal to God and who was not.

Moses stood at the gateway to the camp and said, 'Whoever is for God, join me!' – and all the Levites gathered around him. (Exodus 32:26).

At a time when allegiance to God was being tested, the Levites distinguished themselves. It is appropriate for them to be rewarded with a special relationship with God. Furthermore, based on what we have written above, it is safe to say that those who were most to blame for the sin of the Golden Calf were the firstborns themselves.

The Bible tells us that the Golden Calf was worshipped with "elevation offerings and peace offerings" (Exodus 32:6). We can safely assume that the firstborns – already seen by the people as serving a priestly role – would have been the officiants of this pagan worship. Furthermore, all the tribal princes were firstborn males. In the culture of that time, the firstborn of a family was an authority figure. Clearly, if the people collectively committed such a grave sin, the firstborns – the natural and accepted leadership of the community – ought to bear primary responsibility.

If the status of the firstborns was stripped, why was it necessary to redeem them for five silver shekels? God could simply have stated that He has stripped the firstborns of their special status and bestowed it on the Levites. Furthermore, why does the Bible command us to continue the ceremonial redemption of non-Levite firstborns to this day?

I would like to suggest that the redemption of firstborns serves a very important purpose. Any class system in a society is a recipe for internecine strife. When this class system is defined exclusively by family lineage, the possibility of such strife is enhanced. The redemption of every firstborn male in Israel serves as a perpetual reminder of the origins of the special status of the Levites. Every time a firstborn is redeemed, we are reminded that, ideally, all families and tribes were to be of equal status. The tribe of Levi did not come by their status unjustly. They did not take it through force or political manipulation. They earned this status by answering Moses' call and by demonstrating their devotion to God in a time of crisis.

At the same time, the firstborns, who remain the leaders of their tribes and families, are reminded of a time of failed leadership. As leaders of the community, they are forever reminded that leadership is correctly bestowed on those who answer the call, "Whoever is for God, join me!"

Naso

Numbers 4:21-7:89

When God "Shines His Face" Towards Us

I N THE PORTION of the Bible, Naso, we find the priestly blessing, the three verses that God commanded the *Kohanim*, the priests from the family of Aaron, to recite when blessing the children of Israel. Each of the three verses is made up of two statements. I'd like to examine the second verse of the three closely.

The Lord shall shine His face towards you and be gracious to you. (Numbers 6:25).

This verse tells us that God will grant two things to the recipients of this blessing.

1. *He will shine His face towards them*
2. *He will be gracious to them*

What exactly does this blessing mean?

The previous verse (Numbers 6:24) described God blessing and protecting those blessed. The word "bless"—*barech*—in that verse usually refers to abundance. The blessings of that verse, abundance, and protection, are easily understood. In this verse, by contrast, the meaning of the blessings is less clear. Here, God promises to "shine His face towards you" and "be gracious to you."

What does it mean for God to "shine His face towards" someone? Does that give them wisdom? Happiness? Success? Strength? Prophetic power? As beautiful as these words are, their precise meaning is unclear. The immediate context of the verse does not provide any clarity on the matter.

The second blessing of this verse, "He shall be gracious to you," is equally unclear, but for a different reason. The Hebrew word used here can be interpreted grammatically in several ways. The Hebrew word for "and He shall be gracious to you" is *vi'chune-ka*. The first syllable, *vi*, is the Hebrew prefix meaning "and." The final syllable, *ka*, means "you." The verb root of the word is *chen*. This root has several possible meanings. To illustrate, two examples, among many in the Bible, use the same root as our word here.

As the eyes of a maid go to the hand of her mistress, so our eyes look to the Lord our God until He has mercy on us. (Psalms 123:2).

And Esther obtained favor in the sight of all who saw her. (Esther 2:15).

In the quote from Psalm 123, the root *chen* means "mercy" or "compassion." However, in the verse from Esther, the meaning of *chen* is "favor," meaning that Esther was admired and liked by other people. There are numerous examples of its root meanings in the scripture. Without getting into the technicalities of Hebrew conjugation, it suffices to say that it is unclear which meaning is correct for our verse.

To sum up this point, the meaning of the root of the word

vi'chuneka – "and He shall be gracious to you" – is either the "grace" or the "favor." Our verse promises that God will show grace and mercy to those being blessed or that He will grant them favor in the eyes of others. It is important to note that both possibilities are equally grammatically correct.

This problem leads us to another question. How would either of these options relate to the first blessing of the verse, "The Lord shall shine His face towards you"?

Excluding our verse, seven verses in the Bible speak of God shining His face. In five of the seven, the context is God's redemption of Israel from exile and oppression at the hands of other nations. Three of these five repeat phrases in the same chapter, Psalm 80.

"Cause Your face to shine, And we shall be saved!"(Psalm 80:3,7,19).

The other two verses that refer to the redemption of Israel are:

Now, our God, hear the prayers and petitions of your servant. For your sake, Lord, look with favor – [lit. "shine Your face"] on your desolate sanctuary. – Daniel 9:17

May God be gracious to us and bless us, and make His face shine on us, so that Your ways may be known on earth, your salvation among all nations. (Psalm 67:1-2).

The remaining two verses, which refer to God shining His face, speak of personal, private redemption from enemies.

Deliver me from the hand of my enemies; And those who persecute me. Make Your face shine upon Your servant; Save me for Your mercies' sake. – Psalm 31:15-16

Redeem me from the oppression of man, That I may keep Your precepts. Make Your face shine upon Your servant, And teach me Your statutes. (Psalm 119:134-135).

In summary, when the Bible describes God shining His face, it means God is saving Israel or an individual from exile or oppression. If we look more closely at these verses, there is another important implication. The redemption of Israel is not a final goal in and of itself. It is meant to bring about the kingdom of God on earth, the redemption of the entire world.

We see this in Daniel, where we find Daniel praying not only to end the exile but for the rebuilding of the Temple in Jerusalem. On the personal level, the verse in Psalm 119 quoted above describes redemption from enemies to be accessible to serve God by keeping the commandments. In other words, when someone in the Bible prays to God to shine His face, the meaning of the prayer is the plea to God for redemption so that the supplicant can proceed to accomplish a higher goal in the service of God.

This implication is most evident in Psalm 67:1:

God be merciful to us and bless us, cause His face to shine upon us, Selah

That Your way may be known on earth, Your salvation among all nations.

Let the people praise You, O God; Let all the people praise You. (Psalm 67:1-3).

As we clearly see, the stated purpose of Israel's redemption is the universal goal of all nations and all peoples praising and worshipping the God of Israel. Keeping in mind that Israel's mission is to bring all humanity to faith in God, we can now return to our verse in Numbers.

I suggest that the meaning of this verse is as follows.

The Lord shall shine His face towards you - God will redeem you from exile and oppression *and be gracious to you.* - and He will grant you favor in the eyes of others so that you can influence them to have faith in the God of Israel.

Seen this way, the second half of the verse should be translated, "and He shall grant you favor." A number of the traditional Jewish commentaries understand the verse this way.

This is an essential lesson for all people of faith. Even as we pray to God to bless and redeem us from trouble and adversaries, we must remember the purpose of the redemption we pray for. When God grants us freedom and elevates us to a position of autonomy and influence, He does so to give us the tools to build His kingdom for all.

Beha'alotecha

The Alternate Storyline in the Book of Numbers

T HERE IS A strange and unique phenomenon in the middle of this week's Bible portion. Two verses, Numbers 10:35-36, are written between an unusual marking in the Bible. Two backward and upside-down *nuns* are actually written into the traditional text of the Bible, one before and one after these two verses. (see accompanying image)

To understand the meaning behind these strange markings in the Bible, let's first look at these two verses more carefully.

"When the Ark traveled, Moses proclaimed, 'Rise up, O God, and Your enemies will scatter and let those who hate You flee from before You.' And when it came to rest, he said, 'Return O God the myriads of Israel's thousands.'" (Numbers 10:35-36).

In the Talmud, the Jewish sages discussed the strange phenomenon of the two backward *nuns*:

The Sages taught: It is stated: "And when the Ark traveled,

Moses proclaimed: Rise up, God, and Your enemies will scatter and let those who hate You flee from before You." The Holy One, Blessed be He, made signs in the Bible for this portion, before and after it, in order to say that this is not its place. Rabbi Judah says: It is not for that reason that signs were inserted. Rather, the signs are there because this portion is considered a book unto itself. – Talmud Shabbat 116a

Upside down and backward letters? A separate book? What does all of this mean?

Perhaps we can understand this peculiarity by answering a different question. What event is described by these verses? According to these two verses, when the people of Israel traveled, the ark would precede them. Moses would utter this declaration, thus causing the enemies of Israel to scatter and flee. Moses would then make a second declaration when the Ark came to rest.

When did this ever occur? Numerous wars between Israel and other nations are recorded in the Bible. There is no conflict that appears to fit the bill. What exactly is being described here?

The book of Numbers leading up to this point describes the ideal setup of the camp of Israel with the flags of each of the tribes, the inauguration of the Tabernacle, and the protocol for travel. The final verse immediately preceding our two verses describes the beginning of the travel of the nation of Israel to the land of Canaan to take possession of it.

We read a series of disturbing stories in the chapters following this two-verse section. The nation of Israel complains about the manna from heaven. The spies sent by Moses return with a negative report about the land, leading the nation to lose faith. Soon thereafter, we read about the tragic rebellion led by Korach and the plague that followed it.

It goes without saying that had everything gone as planned, these problematic episodes would not have occurred. Consider how the story of Israel was supposed to unfold. After the aforementioned setting up of the camp and ceremonies inaugurating the Tabernacle that opens the book of Numbers, the children of Israel were supposed to march northward into the promised Land. God, as promised earlier in the Bible, was going to cause the enemies of Israel to flee before them. The conquest of the land was meant to be miraculous and effortless.

Instead, spies were sent. Trust in the almighty hand of God wavered. The decree of forty years in the desert followed. After forty years, the next generation would conquer the land through natural military means rather than by overt miracles.

The two verses between the backward *nuns* are remarkable because they describe something that never happened. They describe the miraculous defeat of Israel's enemies caused by Moses making a declaration as the ark traveled before the people.

Now, we can understand the cryptic comments of the rabbis in the Talmud. These two verses are not in the right place. This means that they record an event that never actually happened. They are a separate book.

When I was growing up, there were books labeled as "Choose Your Own Adventure." In these books, the reader can decide which direction the plot would take by making choices at critical junctures in the story. If choice A, turn to page X. If choice B, turn to page Y.

I'd like to suggest that these two verses remind us of the unrealized ideal end of the story. At this point in the book of Numbers, the children of Israel, led by Moses and the ark, were meant to march northward into the land, as their enemies miraculously scattered. Instead, they chose the path of rebellion, fear, and loss of faith. For this reason, the two verses are written between the backward *nuns* – a kind of ancient parentheses. They remain in the text of the Bible to remind us of the ideal that could have and should have been realized.

We make many decisions in our lives. After making a wrong turn, we live with our mistakes and cope with the new imperfect reality we have chosen. We must remember that God gives us the opportunity to go back and fix our mistakes.

We can return, repent, and start fresh. Just as these two verses were included in the Bible, although they never happened, many of our lost opportunities can be revived and renewed, and we dare not think that they are gone forever, as the Talmud records later in the discussion of the backward *nuns*.

> *Rabban Shimon ben Gamliel says: In the future, this portion will be uprooted from here, where it appears, and will be written in its proper place. — Talmud Shabbat 116a*

Shelach

Numbers 13:1-15:41

Yehoshua's Protection

THE MAIN NARRATIVE in the portion of the Bible, Shelach, tells the story of the sin of the spies. The children of Israel sent spies to the land of Canaan to scout out the land and report back to the people. The spies came back with a negative report of the promised land. They instilled fear, panic, and despair in the people.

Two of the spies dissented. Caleb and Joshua brought a positive and encouraging report. Joshua was Moses' primary disciple and eventual successor.

Before the spies depart on their mission, their names are listed. Joshua's name is listed as "Hoshe'a, the son of Nun" (13:8). At the conclusion of the list, the Bible states:

> *"These are the names of the men whom Moses sent to scout the land, and Moses called Hoshe'a the son of Nun, Yehoshua." (13:16)*

(From for the duration of this teaching we will refer to Joshua by the Hebrew pronunciation, Yehoshua)

In this verse we are told that Yehoshua's original name was Hoshe'a, and that his name was changed to Yehoshua by Moses. In the Bible, changing a name by one's master is not unique to this situation. For example, in Genesis, Pharaoh changed Joseph's name when he appointed him viceroy over Egypt. (Genesis 41:45).

It is important to note that Yehoshua was already referred to as Yehoshua, the name Moses gave him on a number of occasions earlier in the Bible (see Exodus 17:9-14, 32:17, Numbers 11:28). This leads to an obvious question. If Moses changed his name from Hoshe'a to Yehoshua only now, at the sending of the spies, why was he already called Yehoshua in the earlier passages we mentioned? On the other hand, if Moses made the change at an earlier point, why is the name change mentioned only now?

A number of traditional commentaries assert that the change of name took place here at the time of the sending of the spies. According to this approach, Yehoshua is called by this name earlier is the Bible in reference to how he would be known in the future. There is some logic to this. After all, Joshua would play a central role in the Biblical narrative of the entry and conquest of the land. Keeping his name consistent across all stories about him makes sense. Following this reasoning, he is called Hoshe'a here in the list of the spies in order to present the name change in its proper context at the time the change was made.

Regardless of when the actual change of his name took place, the question remains. What is the connection between this name change and the sending of the spies that warranted its mention here in Numbers 13?

The Talmud (Sotah 34b) comments as follows:

Moses prayed for him [saying] 'May the Lord [Yah] save you from the counsel of the spies.'

The Talmud is making a wordplay with the two-letter name of God, Yah, and the difference in spelling between the two names, Hoshe'a and Yehoshua. In Hebrew, the difference between the two names is only one letter. Hoshe'a is four letters – *heh, vav, shin,* and *ayin.* Yehoshua is the same four letters with a *yud* added at the beginning. The first two letters in Yehoshua are *yud* and *heh* – the same as the two-letter name of God, Yah.

הושע   Hoshe'a

יהושע   Yehoshua

A second aspect of this wordplay is that the name Hoshe'a means "save." Yehoshua means "God saves," with the yud at the beginning referring to God.

This wordplay/prayer of Moses is peculiar. If only a single letter *yud* was added to the four-letter name Hoshe'a, not any full name of God, why does the Talmud suggest that Moses was invoking the name *Yah*? God's most common name YHVH also begins with *yud.* Since only the letter *yud* was added, why did the sages of the Talmud not suggest "May the the Lord (i.e. YHVH) save you ..." as the prayer of Moses? What do the sages single out the name *Yah* in the prayer for Yehoshua to be saved from the negative report of the spies?

This two-letter name for God appears only twice in the Bible. The first is in the song that the children of Israel sang at the time of splitting the Red Sea.

"The strength and retribution of Yah was the cause of my deliverance. This is my God, and I will glorify Him; the God of my father and I will exalt Him." (Exodus 15:2).

The second appearance of *Yah* appears soon after the first, just after the war with Amalek who had attacked the Children of Israel not long after the splitting of the sea.

> *"The Lord said to Moses, 'Write this as a remembrance in the book, and repeat it in Yehoshua's ears, for I will totally obliterate the memory of Amalek from under the heavens.' Moses built an altar and called it the Lord is My Banner. He said, 'For the hand is on the throne of Yah: the Lord maintains a war against Amalek from generation to generation."* (Exodus 17:14-16).

Note the mention of Yehoshua along with the second time *Yah* is used. Yehoshua was the one who led the battle against Amalek.

Looking at these two passages, the only two uses of the name yah in the Bible, we notice an obvious connection. In both passages, the context is the defeat of, or battle against, the enemies of Israel. The first verse, from the song at the Red Sea, refers to the defeat of the Egyptians, and the second refers to the perpetual war with Amalek, the archenemy of Israel.

It is interesting that the 1st-century Aramaic translator of the Bible, Onkelos, translates *Yah* as "fear of God" [*d'chila Hashem*] in the first reference and as "fear of His presence" [*d'chila di'shchinteih*] in the second. It seems that for Onkelos, this name of God, *Yah*, denotes the awesome God who strikes fear in enemies of Israel.

In light of the above, I would like to suggest two ways to understand what the sages of the Talmud meant in their comment about the change from Hoshe'a to Yehoshua.

Onkelos' translation suggests that the name *Yah* connotes fear of God. Reading this into Moses's prayer suggested in the Talmud, Moses prayed for Yehoshua to have an extra dose of fear of God. Fear of God would prevent Yehoshua from reporting anything other than a glowing report about God's chosen land. After all, if God chose it how could there be anything wrong with it?

A second approach would be to look at the name *Yah* in its full meaning and context. Yehoshua was the one who led the battle against Amalek. At the end of that war, we read that

> *Yehoshua weakened Amalek and his people with the edge of the sword. (Exodus 17:13).*

Yehoshua was someone who had tasted victory over the enemies of Israel. He had seen the fear in the eyes of Amalek. He had exacted revenge upon them. To a certain extent, as a result of this experience, Yehoshua possessed the characteristic of *Yah*.

The dispute between Yehoshua, Caleb, as well as the other spies, revolved around whether or not the children of Israel could defeat the Canaanite nations who dwelt in the land.

> *"We came to the land into which you sent us and indeed it flows with milk and honey, and this is its fruit. However, the nation is mighty, and those who inhabit the land and the cities are greatly fortified to the utmost. We also saw the offspring of the giant over there. Amalek dwells in the southern part of the land, the Hittites, Jebusites, and Emorites dwell in the mountain, and the Canaanites dwell by the sea and next to the Jordan."*
>
> *Caleb silenced the people to Moses, and he said: "We can surely go up [to the land] and we shall possess it for we are surely able to overcome it.' But the men who went up with him said: 'We are not able to go up against the nation for they are more powerful than we." (Numbers 13:27-31).*

Put simply, the spies saw mighty nations – they saw Amalek – and they were afraid. Yehoshua and Caleb were not afraid. Here is their report:

> *"The land through which we have passed to scout; the land is very, very good. If the Lord desires us, He will bring us into this land and give it to us, a land that flows with milk and honey. However, do not rebel against the Lord, and you do not be afraid of the nation of the land for they are [as] our bread, their protection is removed from them, and the Lord is with us; do not be afraid of them." (Numbers 14:7-9).*

For Yehoshua, the victor over Amalek, fear of the nations is nonsense. What saved Yehoshua from fear of the nations – the fear that the other spies felt – was the power of *Yah*, that Godly power over the enemies of Israel, the fear of God, which Yehoshua himself had experienced in the victory over Amalek. And it was the fear of God that prevented Yehoshua from fearing the Canaanite nations.

Today, as then, there are nations that seek to prevent the nation of Israel from possessing the land. We must follow the example of Yehoshua and Caleb, who taught us that where there is fear of God, there is nothing else to fear.

Korach

Numbers 16:1–18:32

Incense and the
Copper Overlay

I n the portion of the bible, Korach son of Yizhar of the tribe of Levi, leads a rebellion of two hundred fifty men against God and Moses. In their initial complaint, Korach and his followers attacked Moses and Aaron for seizing power. It goes without saying that Korach did not accept the possibility that God Himself had chosen Moses and Aaron for their leadership roles.

They gathered against Moses and Aaron and said to them, "You have gone too far! For all the community are holy, all of them, and the Lord is in their midst. Why then do you raise yourselves above the Lord's congregation?" (Numbers 16:3).

Moses came up with a public test to refute the rebels' claims.

[Moses] spoke to Korah and all his company, saying, "To-morrow morning the Lord will show who is His and who is holy, and will cause him to come near to Him. That one whom He chooses He will cause to come near to Him. Do

this: Take firepans, Korach, and all your company; put fire in them and put incense in them before the Lord tomorrow, and it shall be that the man whom the Lord chooses is the holy one. You take too much upon yourselves, you sons of Levi!" (Numbers 16:5-7).

Moses instructed all two hundred fifty and Aaron to take firepans and to burn incense to God. As soon as they did this, the response from God was swift and severe.

A fire came forth from God and consumed the two hundred and fifty men who were bringing the incense. (Numbers 16:35).

In the aftermath of this dramatic event, having verified His choice of Moses and Aaron for leadership, God proceeded to give Moses a peculiar instruction.

Speak to Elazar the son of Aaron, the priest, and have him lift up the firepans from the inferno, and scatter the fire yonder, for they were sanctified; the firepans of these sinners [who paid] with their lives, and make them into hammered sheets to overlay the altar. So Elazar, the priest, took the copper firepans that the fire victims brought and hammered them into a covering for the altar. [This was] a reminder for the People of Israel so that a commoner shall never approach – one who is not a descendant of Aaron – to burn incense before the Lord so as not to be like Korach and his congregation. (Numbers 17:2-5).

Here, God instructed Moses that the copper firepans used by the 250 rebels were to be made into a copper overlay for the altar. As God explained, this copper overlay would serve as a permanent reminder that any non-priest is forbidden from bringing an incense offering to God. To better understand the meaning behind God's instruction to Moses, let's first learn a bit more about the altar the hammered copper firepans would be covering.

There were two altars in the Tabernacle. A smaller gold-covered altar inside the sanctuary was used for the daily incense offering. This altar is referred to as the "incense altar" (see Exodus 30:1). A second, much larger altar was in the courtyard, outside the sanctuary. It was upon this altar that portions of the sacrifices and the daily offerings were burnt. It is important to note that this larger altar was to be covered by copper from the firepans, not the incense altar in the sanctuary.

Why is this altar the appropriate venue for a reminder that no non-priest is allowed to bring incense? To answer this question, we must first understand why the offering of incense was chosen as the appropriate test of the rebellious group's validity.

In Leviticus 10, Aaron's two sons, Nadav and Avihu, were killed by God. Their sin was the following.

Nadav and Avihu, Aaron's sons, took, each of them, his firepan, placed fire upon it, and then placed incense upon it, and they brought an alien fire which He had not commanded them. (Leviticus 10:1).

The incense offering is the most intimate service to God. It is incense that is offered in the Holy of Holies on the Day of Atonement, *Yom Kippur*, the holiest day of the year. Incense was the only offering ever brought into the Holy of Holies, the innermost and most sacred place in the Tabernacle. Nadav and Avihu wanted to approach God in the most intimate way. But they attempted to have intimacy with God, which God did not request. Instead of the warmth of God's presence, they were consumed by a deadly fire.

Among the many offerings listed in the Bible, there are offerings that may be brought when a person simply wishes to be close to God, not as atonement for any sin. These are called *shelamim*—peace offerings. A person who desires closeness with God may bring one of these offerings at almost any time. Incense, unlike a peace offering, is more intimate. Similar to interpersonal relationships, intimacy must be invited. Uninvited intimacy is an offensive violation of the relationship.

Korach and his rebels argued that Aaron and Moses should not have special status. They argued that every person in Israel ought to be equivalent.

"for the entire congregation are all holy, and the Lord is in their midst; why do you raise yourselves above the Lord's congregation?'"(Numbers 17:3)

They claimed that it is not right that only Aaron is permitted to serve God in the most intimate way. Israel should be allowed to approach God to serve him equally. Moses' response was that God chose this arrangement, and it is not for us to decide who serves God and in what way. Just because a particular person wants to serve God in a particular way does not suffice to permit the service to be done.

Considering how Nadav and Avihu died, it is clear that Moses chose incense as the test because of this earlier event. The Jewish sages highlight this connection in this Midrashic comment, suggesting Moses' thinking to illustrate this exact point.

Here you have the service that is beloved over all others – the incense which is the beloved of all offerings – but it is poisonous, for with it Nadav and Avihu were burnt. Therefore, he warned [the rebels], 'It shall be that the man that God

shall choose is the holy one.(Numbers 16:7) – Midrash Bam-
idbar Rabbah 18:8

The deadly lesson was that it is God, and only God, who sets the parameters of our relationship. We dare not violate God's boundaries when they appear unfair or because we fail to understand them.

As explained earlier, the outer altar – the one that was to be overlaid with the copper from the firepans – stood in the courtyard. It was on this altar that all offerings were burnt. While a non-priest was permitted to enter this courtyard to bring an offering, he was not allowed to ascend the altar. (This altar was very large and had a ramp to carry up the offerings to be burnt.) A non-priest was not allowed to go beyond the courtyard in front of this altar. Beyond this altar was the sanctuary, which contained the Menorah, the Table, and the Incense Altar. Beyond the sanctuary was the Holy of Holies, which contained the Ark of the Covenant.

It follows that the Menorah, Table, Incense Altar, and Ark were almost never seen by any non-priest. The altar in the courtyard was the point beyond which the non-priest was forbidden to go. He was not even allowed to bring his own offering up the ramp to the top of the altar. For this reason, the outer altar was actually the ideal place for a reminder of the rebellion of Korach.

Any time a non-priest approached the large altar, he saw the copper overlay. This overlay would remind him of the incident of the rebellion of Korach and the 250 men. He would thus be reminded, lest he question the rules and his own place in the hierarchy, that God alone sets the boundaries.

The message of the copper overlay made from the rebels' firepans is twofold. First, we are reminded that God ordains different roles for different people. We must humbly accept that we each have our role to play, and we must be careful not to allow our egos to cause us to question God's choices, as Korach did. Second, the copper overlay reminds us that we worship Him on God's terms—and not our own.

Chukat

Numbers 19:1–22:1

A Better Complaint

I N THIS WEEK'S Torah portion, we read about the death of Miriam, the prophetess sister of Moses and Aaron. Immediately following her death, the water ceased flowing from the rock (Numbers 20:1-2). The people complained to Moses.

> *The people thus contended with Moses and spoke, saying, "If only we had perished when our brothers perished before the Lord! Why, then, have you brought the Lord's assembly into this wilderness for us and our beasts to die here? Why have you made us come up from Egypt to bring us into this wretched place? It is not a place of grain or figs or vines or pomegranates, nor is there water to drink." (Numbers 20:3-5).*

God told Moses and Aaron to speak to the rock in the presence of the people, and the water would begin flowing again.

> *Moses and Aaron gathered the assembly before the rock. And he said to them, "Listen now, you rebels; shall we bring forth water for you out of this rock?" Then Moses lifted up his hand*

*and struck the rock twice with his rod, and water came forth
abundantly, and the congregation and their beasts drank. But
the Lord said to Moses and Aaron, "Because you have not
believed Me, to treat Me as holy in the sight of the sons of Israel, therefore you shall not bring this assembly into the land
which I have given them." (Numbers 20:10-12).*

Instead of speaking to the rock as God instructed, Moses hit
the rock. Notice that in His rebuke of Moses and Aaron, God
makes no mention of hitting the rock. Furthermore, what exactly did God mean that Moses and Aaron did not "treat Me as
holy in the sight" of the people of Israel?

To solve this question, we must understand the overall structure of the Book of Numbers. A few weeks ago, we read the story
of the spies (ch. 13-14). Because the people lacked faith in God
and accepted the negative report of the spies, God decreed that
they would spend forty years in the desert, during which all those
above the age of 20 at the time of the sin would die. This story
took place just over a year after the Exodus.

Next, we have the rebellion of Korach and his followers (last
week's Torah portion). The Korach rebellion is followed by two
sets of laws. First is a list of the various tithes and gifts due to
the Levites and priests. This list follows the rebellion because
Korach's argument was that all the people are equally holy and
that Moses and Aaron had usurped their special status for themselves (see last week's column). Reinforcement of the Levitical
and priestly hierarchy in the wake of the rebellion makes sense.

These laws are followed by chapter 19, the beginning of this
week's Torah portion. Chapter 19 records the laws of impurity
imparted by contact with human death and the ritual procedure
for purification from it. Why is this chapter here? It would make
more sense to find it in Leviticus, along with the other rules of

impurities and purification. It almost seems that this chapter was cut out from Leviticus and inserted here. Why?

We can answer this question by paying careful attention to the details of chapter 20. After Miriam's death and the scene of the rock hitting, we read about Israel traveling towards the promised land. Later in the chapter, we read about Aaron's death.

Although not explicitly stated, it is clear that these events took place in the final year of the forty years in the desert. The Bible explicitly states that Aaron died in the desert in the fortieth year (Numbers 33:38).

To sum up. Numbers 20 took place in the fortieth and final year. The previous story, the Korach rebellion and its aftermath, happened just over a year after the Exodus. In other words, Numbers 19, impurity and purification from human death, appears at the point of transition from the second year to the fortieth. The placement of this section here is now clear. For forty years, the children of Israel were camped in the desert, waiting for God's decree to come to an end. All who were over the age of 20 at the time of the sin of the spies would have to die. None would enter the land except for Joshua and Caleb. As a subtle hint that this era of death and dying was now over, the Torah inserted the rules for purification from death at this precise point.

With all this in mind, let's return to our original issue. What exactly did Moses and Aaron do wrong? Let's reread the people's complaint.

The people thus contended with Moses and spoke, saying, "If only we had perished when our brothers perished before the Lord! Why, then have you brought the Lord's assembly into this wilderness, for us and our beasts to die here? Why have you made us come up from Egypt to bring us into this wretched place? It is not a place of grain or figs or grapes or pomegranates, nor is there water to drink." (Numbers 20:3-5).

Compare this to an earlier complaint.

the children of Israel wept again and said, "Who will give us meat to eat? We remember the fish that we used to eat for free in Egypt, the cucumbers and the melons and the leeks and the onions and the garlic, but now our appetite is gone. There is nothing at all to look at except this manna." – (Numbers 11:4-6).

Notice the foods mentioned. In the complaint from Numbers 11, they recalled the foods they ate in Egypt. And as opposed to Numbers 20, there is no mention of God. But here in Numbers 20, grain? Figs? Grapes? Pomegranates?

This reminds us of the description of the land of Israel in Deuteronomy.

A land of wheat and barley, of vines and fig trees and pomegranates, a land of olive oil and honey; - (Deuteronomy 8:8).

The earlier generation complained that they missed the menu in Egypt. Forty years later, the complaint is completely different. Rather than longing for a return to Egypt, this new generation wants to enter the land of Israel!

Perhaps we can now understand another dimension to Moses' mistake. When Moses was approached by the people complaining about the lack of water, he understood it as a replay of their parents' complaints. And he treated the complaints the same way. He called the people "rebels," and he hit the rock, repeating what had been done forty years earlier.

What Moses failed to see was this generation was different. They did not want a return to Egypt. They were not afraid to enter the land. They had no lack of faith. In fact, in the next chapter, we read of multiple military victories as they began their approach to the promised land.

Perhaps God deemed Moses and Aaron unsuitable to lead the nation into the land because they failed to see the strength and faith of this new generation. The lesson is important for all of us. We often make the mistake of seeing new situations through old lenses. We hold on to outdated assumptions and are blinded to positive changes and new realities that God has placed before us. We must trust that God will always raise up exactly who He needs to lead His people to the promised land.

Balak

Numbers 22:2–25:9

Tents of Jacob, Tabernacles of Israel

I N THE PORTION of the Bible, Balak, we learn about Balaam, who was hired by the Moabite king *Balak* to curse Israel. God initially told Balaam that he must not go with the men to curse Israel. Later, God told Balaam to go with Balak's men and to say whatever He would tell Balaam to say. The result was that Balaam ended up blessing Israel instead of cursing them.

I'd like to discuss one verse from Balaam's Blessings.

"How beautiful are your tents, Jacob, your tabernacles, Israel!"(Numbers 24:5).

The Hebrew word translated here as "your tabernacles" is *mishkanotecha*. Many English translations render it as "your dwellings." While this translation is accurate, of the 140 times the word *mishkan* – "tabernacle" or "dwelling" - appears in the Bible, approximately 120 of them refer explicitly to the Tabernacle or the Tent of Meeting in the desert. So, while it makes sense to translate *mishkan* in our verse as "dwelling," the word carries with it the connotation of the Tabernacle, God's dwelling place, the house of worship.

In this blessing, Balaam refers to the nation of Israel by the common name, *Israel*, but also as *Jacob*. The name *Jacob* is used collectively for the people of Israel on many occasions. To understand the deeper meaning of our verse, we first need to explore what *Jacob* means by referring to the entire nation.

The meaning of Jacob's name is explained twice in Genesis. First, when Jacob is born, his name is explained as a reference to his grasping the heel of his brother Esau at the moment of birth (Genesis 25:26). The Hebrew word for the heel is akev. The word for "follow" is akav from the same root. "Jacob"—Ya'akov—*followed* his brother out of the womb, grasping his *heel*. Therefore, he was named *Ya'akov*, Jacob.

Later, after Jacob and his mother Rebekah deceived his father Isaac so that Jacob would receive the birthright blessings, Esau unjustly accused Jacob of cheating him, despite the fact that Jacob had earlier purchased the birthright from Esau, entitling him to these blessings. When Esau realized that Jacob had "stolen" the blessings, Esau gave Jacob's name a new meaning.

Esau said, "Is he not rightly named Jacob? For he has cheated me these two times. He took away my birthright, and behold, now he has taken away my blessing." (Genesis 27:36).

The Hebrew word for "cheated" here is akav, which comes from the same root as Jacob's name. It implies lying in wait, ambushing, or deceiving.

Simply put, the name "Jacob" does not have positive connotations. It variously implies *following*, *being on the heel*, *deception*, and *cheating*. In fact, if we look at Jacob's own life, we see that he was often compelled to live by his wits and outsmart others - whether it was Laban, Esau, or even his own father. Jacob, unlike his father Isaac and grandfather Abraham, lived much of his life in exile under the authority of others.

What is true of Jacob as an individual is true of his offspring – the Jewish people. This is why they are sometimes referred to collectively as *Jacob*. The Jewish people, like their forefathers and namesake, are sometimes forced to live in exile as subordinates and second-class citizens – the *follower*, the *heel* - in hostile and oppressive environments. Like Jacob, their father, Jews have repeatedly been forced to flee after being unjustly accused and targeted. And so, when scripture refers to the People of Israel as *Jacob*, this subordinate, exile identity is being described. For example:

> *"For the Lord will deliver Jacob and redeem them from the hand of those stronger than they." (Jeremiah 31:11).*

We see this, as well, where God is referred to as "the God of Jacob."

> *May the Lord answer you in the day of trouble! May the name of the God of Jacob protect you! - (Psalm 20:2).*

> *The nations rage, the kingdoms totter; he utters his voice, and the earth melts. The Lord of hosts is with us; the God of Jacob is our fortress. (Psalm 46:6-7).*

Day of trouble? The nation's rage? The God of *Jacob* protects and shields His people when they are being attacked, pursued, and persecuted by the nations. (See also Psalms 76:7, 84:9, 94:7, 75:10, 81:2,5)

But Jacob has another name: *Israel*. He was given a second, more honorable, and loftier name when he wrestled with and defeated the angel who attacked him. (Genesis 32:29) He won a battle not through deception but through prayer and direct physical struggle. For this victory, he was told that he was now capable of truly triumphing. He would now be *Yisrael*, derived from two words: *sar* – meaning "prince" or "minister," and *el*, meaning "God" or "power."

Yet he retained both of his names. Sometimes, he would need to be Jacob, living by his wits as a second-class citizen in a hostile and anti-Semitic environment. At other times, he would be able to behave as Israel—triumphant, influential, and strong.

Now to Balaam's blessing:

"How beautiful are your tents, Jacob, your tabernacles, Israel!" (Numbers 24:5).

It is interesting that Balaam connects "tents" to "Jacob" and "tabernacles" to "Israel." The first half of the verse describes Jacob and Esau as young men.

So the boys grew. Esau was a skillful hunter and a man of the field, but Jacob was a mild man who drew in tents. (Genesis 25:27).

Tents are homes. They are private places. "Your tents, Jacob". Jacob describes a private, inward focus in our relationship to God. Any devoted servant of God confronts challenges on a daily basis. It may be true that the primary task in serving God is to influence, to lead, and to help others get close to Him. But with influence comes interaction. It is impossible to repair the world without engaging with it. And with that engagement, people of faith all too often find themselves in the position of being influenced by the darker parts of the world rather than changing them for the better.

For this, we need to be, like Jacob, "dwellers of tents." To stay strong in one's religious values and continue to influence the world for the good, we must also retreat from it. We must travel inward to our homes, to our families, to our tents.

A *tabernacle*, on the other hand, is very public. The entire purpose of a tabernacle is the glory of God. It is open to all to enter to worship and be inspired. The covenantal relationship's higher calling with God is about the Tabernacle. Anyone who has faith in God and devotes their life to serving Him understands that the focus of that mission is to bring knowledge of God to the entire earth. *Israel* is a name that implies this mission. – God. *Israel* connotes the ministering influencing role of God's people.

With all this in mind, we can now fully understand Balaam's blessing. First, Balaam praised Jacob's tents. He praised the way the nation of Israel focuses inward, on their families and their own relationship to God. Then he praised the tabernacles of Israel, the way that Israel fulfils its ministering role, serving as a vehicle to bring all nations into faith and worship of the God of Israel.

Pinchas

Numbers 25:10–30:1

To These Shall the Land be Divided

I N THE PORTION of the Bible, Phineas opens with the reward of
Phineas by God for killing Zimri ben Salu, leader of a family
from the tribe of Simeon, and Kozbi bat Zur, a woman from a
noble Midianite family. Zimri and Kozbi were publicly fornicat-
ing while participating in a pagan orgy in the worship of Baal
Peor. This orgy was initiated by the daughters of Moab, luring
the men of Israel into this immoral pagan debauchery.

Immediately after the reward of Phineas, God spoke to Moses:

*The Lord spoke to Moses, saying, "Be hostile towards the Mid-
ianites and smite them; for they have been hostile to you with
their tricks, with which they have deceived you in the affair
of Peor and in the affair of Cozbi, the daughter of the leader
of Midian, their sister who was slain on the day of the plague
because of Peor." (Numbers 25:16-18).*

This makes sense. The Midianites caused the immorality and
subsequent plague that befell the men of Israel. Now, God wants

Moses to take revenge on the Midianites. Immediately following this instruction to wage war on Midian, God commanded
Moses to take a census.

> *Then it came about after the plague that the Lord spoke to*
> *Moses and to Eleazar the son of Aaron the priest, saying, "Take*
> *a census of all the congregation of the sons of Israel from twenty*
> *years old and upward, by their fathers' households, whoever is*
> *able to go out to war in Israel." (Numbers 26:1-2).*

While the purpose of the census is not explicitly stated here, it
is clear from the context that the goal was to determine the size
of the nation's potential fighting force. God had just commanded Moses to wage war against Midian, and now He told him to
count "whoever is able to go out to war in Israel."

In light of this apparently straightforward purpose of the
census, to count men of fighting age, it is curious to read what
God told Moses immediately after the census was completed.

> *These are the counted of the children of Israel, six hundred*
> *one thousand seven hundred and thirty. Then the Lord spoke*
> *to Moses, saying, "To these, the land shall be divided for an*
> *inheritance according to the number of names. To the greater*
> *in number, you shall increase its inheritance; to the lesser in*
> *number, you shall decrease its inheritance. Each according to its*
> *number shall its inheritance be given." (Numbers 26:51-54).*

Here, God told Moses that the numbers arrived at in this
census would serve as the basis for the size of the portions to be
allotted to each family in the division of the land of Israel. From
this, it seems that the purpose of the census was twofold. First,
as indicated by the context and content of the initial command,

the census aimed to determine the number of potential soldiers to fight a war against Midian. Then, at the end of the census, God revealed a second purpose, namely, to determine the size of the portions of territory in the promised land.

It seems that God was killing two birds with one stone. Counting men of fighting age had immediate practical value. Once this count was done, God told Moses that this same census could accomplish a second purpose as well.

There are two problems with this explanation. First, when the war against Midian eventually took place, Moses instructed the tribes to contribute one thousand men per tribe, twelve thousand in all. Considering this, what would be the point of counting all six hundred thousand men in preparation for this war? The second difficulty with the 'killing two birds with one stone' explanation is that it is strange. If one of the two purposes of the census was to determine the allotment of territory in the land, why was this not indicated at the outset? Why did God withhold this information until after the census was complete?

I'd like to suggest a straightforward explanation. The purpose of the census was exactly what was stated at the outset. Moses was to count the fighting men of Israel, "whoever is able to go out to war in Israel." In Hebrew, *kol yotze tzava*, literally "all who join the army of Israel."

At the conclusion of the census, God taught Moses and us a powerful lesson: Those who are willing to fight for the land are worthy of inheriting it. To put this another way, the census counted "all who join the army of Israel." Period. If someone were to then ask about how we are to determine the allotment of portions in the land of Israel, God's answer would be simple.

"To these, the land shall be divided for an inheritance according to the number of names.")Numbers 26:53).

Who are "these"? *All who join the army of Israel.* By presenting the dual purpose of the census this way, we learn a lesson that applies at all times. Inheritance of the land requires the willingness to fight and to sacrifice. A people who are unwilling to join the army and fight will never inherit the land and will never be a sovereign nation.

God's promises of the future, the "promised land" that we all strive for, need to be fought for. We must be willing to step up and offer ourselves to the "army of Israel." The promised land's inheritance comes to those willing to fight for it.

Matot

Numbers 30:2-32:42

The Two Vengeances

"God spoke to Moses saying, 'Take vengeance for the Children of Israel against the Midianites; afterward you will be gathered unto your people.' Moses spoke to the people saying, 'Arm men from among yourselves for the legion that they may be against Midian to inflict God's vengeance against Midian.'" (Numbers 31:2-3).

The Midianites had initiated a pagan orgy that led directly to the deaths of twenty-four thousand Israelites. In these verses, God commanded Moses to take vengeance for this tragedy. In God's command, he referred to the vengeance as "vengeance for the Children of Israel." Yet, when Moses relayed the command to the people, he called it "God's vengeance." Why did Moses change the command language?

The great 15th-century commentator Rabbi Don Isaac Abarbanel offers a fascinating insight.

> *"In one instance, this war is referred to as 'vengeance for the Children of Israel,' and in another instance, it refers to it as*

'God's vengeance.' This is because their daughters perpetrated two evils. One is that they caused the deaths of twenty-four thousand from Israel. The second is that they incited them and brought them to idolatry in the service of Pe'or. In reference to the deaths in the plague, the text called [the war] 'vengeance for the Children of Israel', for it is the vengeance for the people. In reference to the idolatry that they served, it is referred to as 'God's vengeance'"

According to Abarbanel, the two acts of vengeance represent two aspects of the damage inflicted by the Midianites. God told Moses that the primary reason for the vengeance was the deaths of twenty-four thousand of His precious people. Moses chose to emphasize the incitement to idolatry, the affront to God.

God, so to speak, is more concerned with the deaths of twenty-four thousand people than with His own honor. At the same time, the children of Israel are taking vengeance for the insult done to God.

This idea that God is concerned with the honor due to Israel, while Israel is concerned with the honor due to God, brings to mind a comment by the 19th-century Lithuanian rabbinic leader, Rabbi Naftali Tzvi Yehuda Berlin, in his commentary to the Passover Haggadah, the liturgy for the Passover Seder. Rabbi Berlin points out that in the Bible, the seven-day festival that we call "Passover" is always referred to as *chag hamatzot*, "the feast of unleavened bread." Rabbi Berlin suggests that God named the festival of the Exodus from Egypt after the matza, the unleavened bread, because of the role the unleavened bread played in the story of the Exodus. Exodus 12:39 relates that the children of Israel rushed out of Egypt and did not have time to bake leavened bread. Calling the festival "the feast of unleavened bread" is a reminder of the haste with which the children of Israel departed Egypt. We, on the other hand, call the festival "Passover," recalling what God did for us as he passed over the homes of the children of Israel while smiting the Egyptian firstborns. The message, Rabbi Berlin explains is that God honors Israel while Israel honors God.

Back to our passage here, Matot, Rabbi Chaim ben Attar (18th century) in his classic commentary *Or Hachaim*, suggests that Moses changed "the vengeance of the children of Israel" to "the vengeance of God" as a way of reminding the children of Israel that any success they have on the battlefield is from God and not the product of their own strength. In other words, according to Or Hachaim, Moses changed the description of vengeance so that the children of Israel would not view the subsequent victory as their own but God's.

Rashi, the greatest of all commentators (11th century), suggests yet another meaning behind Moses's decision.

Whoever attacks Israel is as though he attacks the Holy One blessed be He.

Rashi's comment, that those who attack Israel are attacking God, remains true to this day. In a time when God's biblical promises of the return of the nation of Israel to our homeland after a lengthy exile are being fulfilled, the enemies of Israel must reject the truth of God and His covenantal promises. To oppose Israel's right to be an independent nation in our homeland at this point in history, one must deny the truth of God's word. The enemies of Israel are truly the enemies of God Himself.

In addition to the commentaries I have shared, I'd like to suggest another approach to the two acts of vengeance. While it appears that Moses is changing the word of God, upon closer analysis, he is actually elaborating. It is true that twenty-four thousand Israelites died as a result of what the Midianites did. But what truly caused these deaths was the participation by the children of Israel in sinful pagan behavior. While God emphasized the tragedy that occurred, i.e., the deaths, Moses emphasized the cause of the tragedy.

Perhaps Moses's intent was to rebuke the people at the same time as he was instructing them of God's desire for revenge. While commanding them to take revenge for the deaths, he reminded them that it was their own weakness, their own giving into their desires, that led to the deaths of twenty-four thousand of their brethren.

Idolatry is one of three prohibitions that one must die rather than commit. With this knowledge we may understand Moses's message as follows. God is upset about the deaths of twenty-four thousand Jews. On the other hand, were we to embrace idolatry, we would forfeit the value of our lives. After all, death is preferable to the commission of an idolatrous act. To send this message, Moses altered the language of God's command for vengeance. The true value in our lives is found in our dedication to God.

Masei

Numbers 33:1–36:13

Elim - The Challenge of Comfort

Here are the stages in the Israelites' journey when they came out of Egypt in divisions under the leadership of Moses and Aaron (Numbers 33:1).

THE PORTION OF Masei opens with God commanding Moses to record the more than forty locations where the children of Israel camped during their forty-year journey in the desert. Other than the list of places, this lengthy list has almost no information. Most of these places were not even the location of any significant event along the way. And even when most of the places where significant events occurred appear in the list, the events are not mentioned. One notable exception is a place called Elim.

They moved from Marah and came to Elim. At Elim were twelve springs of water and seventy palm trees, so they camped there. (Numbers 33:9).

The textual question is obvious. Of all the details relating to the dozens of stops along the journey that were omitted, why were these details—the number of plam trees and springs of water—included in this list at the end of the Book of Numbers? To answer this question, we need to understand the significance of Elim to the Exodus narrative. This takes us back to Exodus 15-17.

A series of events are recorded in the two chapters after the splitting of the Red Sea.

- Israel travels for three days and cannot find drinkable water. Moses performs a miracle that sweetens the water. (Exodus 15:22-25).
- They travel and complain that they have no food. God sends Quail and Manna from heaven. (Exodus 16:1-18).
- They travel and again complain about having no water to drink. God tells Moses to hit a rock to bring forth water. (Exodus 17:2-6).

This section is made up of a complaint about water, a complaint about food, and another complaint about water. After the first water complaint and just before the food complaint, the following verse appears:

They came to Elim, where there were twelve springs of water and seventy date palms. They camped by the water. (Exodus 15:27).

Right between a complaint about lack of water and a complaint about lack of food, they camp in a place that is abundant in both water and food! And we must ask, what is the significance of the number of date palms and springs?

It is important to note that all the complaints in this series are interpreted by Moses and God as crises of faith. But is this fair? Why should a complaint that there is no water be understood as a lack of faith in God? If there is no water, why not take the complaint at face value?

It's important to note that the children of Israel were not criticized for their first water complaint. They were simply told after the water had been sweetened, that they must believe in and be obedient to God.

"If you diligently obey the voice of the Lord your God, and do what is upright in His eyes, give ear to His commandments and keep all His statutes, then every sickness that I brought upon Egypt I will not bring upon you, for I am the Lord who heals you." (Exodus 15:26).

At this point, they travel to Elim -the place with the date palms and the springs. *Mechilta deRabi Yishmael* – a Midrash from the second temple era, comments on the significance of the numbers – seventy date palms and twelve springs.

Rabi Elazar HaModai says: On the very day that the Holy One Blessed is He created His world, He created there twelve springs, corresponding to the twelve tribes of Israel, and seventy palm trees corresponding to the seventy elders. - Masechta VaYasa 2

Not only were the people's needs provided for at Elim, but the precise number of trees and springs made it obvious that this place was designed by God specifically for the People of Israel. This, like the scenes before and after it, was a test of the people's faith.

After they complain about the water and God solves the crisis,

He provides the people with the perfect place. All their needs are filled in this unique custom-made oasis. After experiencing such a bountiful and explicit blessing from God, they are once again placed in a situation where their needs are lacking. How they react to this second crisis will reveal the extent to which they learned a lesson from their stay in Elim.

Now we can understand why the twelve springs and seventy palms were included, forty years later, in the list of all the places where Israel camped. The entire purpose of the list is to recall the forty-year journey that is now coming to a close. Moses wanted to remind the people that God took care of them along the way. The one place that most represented this lesson, that God had their needs in mind at all times, is Elim, the custom-made oasis.

When basic needs are lacking, it is all too easy to complain and have a crisis of faith. When we feel that God has not done His part for us, many of us wonder as our ancestors did, "Is God among us or not?" (Exodus 17:7).

On the other hand, when all of our needs are provided for, and life is as it should be, we scarcely notice. After they left Elim and wanted food, the People of Israel did not say, "Well, God provided for us perfectly in the last place. He's obviously taking care of us." The fact that their crisis of faith persists – and even intensifies – after their stay in Elim shows how little they learned from their stay there.

Like at Elim, God often gives us exactly what we need, and we don't appreciate it. If we are going to blame God for the bad times, we must acknowledge that He is also responsible for the good times.

Deuteronomy

Devarim

Deuteronomy 1:1-3:22

Moses, the Rock, and the Spies

THE BOOK OF Deuteronomy is made up of a series of speeches that Moses delivered in the final five weeks of his life. In the opening speech, Moses retold the story of the sin of the spies. As we recall from Numbers 13 and 14, the spies were sent to scout out the land, brought back a negative report, and led the people into a state of despair and panic. As a result of this display of lack of faith, God decreed that the entire generation, all those over the age of twenty, would die over the course of forty years in the desert.

In his review of these events here at the beginning of Deuteronomy, Moses added the following:

> *Also at me was the Lord angry because of you, saying, 'You, too, will not arrive there. Joshua, the son of Nun, who will attend to you, will arrive there. (Deuteronomy 1:37-38).*

Here, when recalling the punishment of the people of Israel, Moses included the decree that Moses himself would not be allowed into the land. This is difficult to understand. The reason for Moses being forbidden from entering the land is well-known. In Numbers 20, in the fortieth year of the sojourn in the desert, God commanded Moses and Aaron to speak to the rock to bring forth water.

> *Then Moses lifted his hand and struck the rock twice with his rod, and water came out abundantly, and the congregation and their animals drank. Then the Lord spoke to Moses and Aaron, "Because you did not believe Me, to hallow Me in the eyes of the children of Israel, therefore you shall not bring this assembly into the land which I have given them." (Numbers 20: 11-12).*

Moses and Aaron were punished for hitting the rock to bring forth water instead of speaking to it. The decree that Moses and Aharon would not be allowed to enter the land of Israel is expressly stated as a punishment for this sin, not for the sin of the spies thirty-eight years earlier.

Furthermore, a close look at the verses in Deuteronomy chapter one indicates that Moses claimed here that God decreed this punishment at the same time as he decreed that the entire generation would not enter the land in the wake of the sin of the spies. This is difficult because Moses's rock-hitting incident occurred thirty-eight years later. Yet here in Deuteronomy 1, the implication is that Moses was forbidden from entering the land of Israel as a result of the sin of the spies.

To sum up, in Numbers 20, we see that God decreed that Moses would not enter the promised land because he struck the rock to bring forth water rather than speaking to it as God commanded. Yet, here in Deuteronomy, Moses claims that he was forbidden from entering the land due to the sin of the spies. How do we solve this problem?

What is the connection between the sin of the spies and the sin of the hitting of the rock? The Kli Yakar explains as follows. A miracle had to be performed to draw water from the rock because the people lacked proper faith. This is evidenced by the fact that God was upset at Moses and Aharon for not maximizing the sanctification of God's name by speaking to the rock. If the people had perfect faith in God they would not have complained the way they did, and a miraculous public display would not have been necessary.

The 16th-century commentator Rabbi Ephraim Luntshitz (*Kli Yakar*) addresses the question. He explains that the sin of the spies was due to a lack of faith. The spies were failed leaders who caused the people to despair. Moses explicitly stated this here in Deuteronomy in his review of the episode 5 verses earlier:

Yet, for all that, you did not have faith in the Lord your God (Deuteronomy 1:32).

God said that He would give Israel the land. The people thought that this was not possible. God's first reaction to the sin of the spies expressed this.

The Lord said to Moses, 'Until when will these people provoke Me, and how much longer will they have no faith in Me, despite all the signs which I have done in their midst.'" (Numbers 14:11).

Because of their lack of faith in God, that generation was doomed to die in the desert.

Thirty-eight years later, the lack of water in the desert provided an opportunity to restore the next generation's faith by performing another "sign in their midst." By hitting the rock instead of speaking to it, Moses did not produce the maximum miracle possible and thus did not completely restore the people's faith. This misstep by Moses allowed the lack of faith that was initiated by the spies to continue.

Rabbi Luntshitz's approach does not entirely answer the question. Why is Moses at fault for all of this? Why is this enough of a reason to suggest that he was punished for the sin of the spies? What does all this have to do with leading the people into the promised land?

In his review of the events surrounding the sin of the spies, Moses mentioned not only that he would not be allowed into the land of Israel but also that his punishment is directly connected to Joshua's choice to lead the people into the land.

Also at me was the Lord angry because of you, saying, 'You, too, will not arrive there. Joshua, the son of Nun, who attends you, will arrive there. (Deuteronomy 1:37-38).

Moses and Joshua had very different reactions to the sin of the spies. After the negative report of the spies and the ensuing panic, the Bible relates Moses's reaction:

Moses and Aharon fell on their faces before the entire gathering of the congregation of the People of Israel." (Numbers 14:5).

Contrast that with Joshua's reaction:

Joshua the son of Nun and Caleb, the son of Jefuneh – tore their garments. They said: "If the Lord desires us, He will bring us into this land and give it to us. However, do not rebel against the Lord…" (Numbers 14:6,8-9).

Joshua's reaction was to implore the people not to lose faith. Moses's reaction was to all upon his face in despair at the people's lack of faith.

Thirty-eight years later, Moses did not maximize the faith of Israel that could have been produced by speaking to the rock as God had commanded him.

Entry into the land of Israel required great faith on the part of the people. This project would entail fourteen years of battle to conquer the land. One of the primary characteristics required for the leader of this military campaign is faith in the people that he is leading. Perhaps Moses's initial reaction to the sin of the spies and his motive for hitting the rock, display that Moses – as great a leader as he was for the People of Israel in the desert – displayed some measure of lack of confidence in the people's faith. This lack of faith prevented him from leading them into the land.

Leaders must have faith in the people they lead. A leader who loses faith in his people's faith cannot lead them to the promised land.

Va'etchanan

Deuteronomy 3:23–7:11

The Chosen People: Chosen for What?

O NE OF THE most common phrases used to describe the People of Israel is "The Chosen People." This idea is first mentioned in this week's Bible portion. The term "chosen" was not used for the people of Israel until this point.

> *Because he loved your forefathers, He chose his descendants after him; and He took you out before Him with his great strength from Egypt. (Deuteronomy 4:37).*

To be "chosen" means to be singled out. But the purpose for which God chose Israel is not mentioned. The obvious question, then, is, "chosen for what?" A few chapters later, this question is answered when this idea is mentioned for the second time.

> *For you are a holy people to the Lord, your God; the Lord, your God, chose you to be for Him a treasured people [heb. 'am segula'] from all the peoples that are on the face of the earth. (Deuteronomy 7:6).*

The answer is that Israel is chosen to be a "treasured people." The Hebrew term *segula*, translated here as "treasured," appears four times in the Bible, the five books of Moses. In all four instances, segula describes the people of Israel. The first time the word appears is in Exodus 19, as God introduced the covenant at Sinai.

"Now, if you will obey Me faithfully and keep My covenant, you shall be for me a treasured possession (heb. 'segula') from among all the peoples, for all the earth is Mine. And you shall be a kingdom of priests and a holy nation for Me." These are the words that you shall speak to the children of Israel.(Exodus 19:5-6).

The great commentator Rabbi Moses Nachmanides (13th century Spain) explains the phrase as follows:

You shall be for me a 'segula' from all the nations: that you shall be a treasure in my hand like a beautiful object that the king will not give into the hand of others. (see Ecclesiastes 2:8). Or 'segula' may mean cleaving [or closeness]." - Nachmanides on the Bible, Exodus 19:5

According to Nachmanides, to be "treasured" means to be beautiful, dear, and closely guarded. Based on this, the meaning of *am segula* – "treasured people" is that the people of Israel are a nation that is dear to God and that He guards closely.

The greatest of all commentators, Rashi (11th century France), further develops this idea.

Segula: A favored [or beloved] treasury as in 'and the treasure of kings and provinces' (Ecclesiastes 2:8) [i.e.] expensive vessels and precious stones that kings store away.(Rashi, Exodus 19:5).

Rabbenu Bachya ibn Pakuda (14th century Spain) adds the following comment:

That which is hidden, covered, and concealed from the eye is called 'segula'. (Commentary on Exodus 19:5

From all the above classical Jewish commentaries, we see that the term *am segula*—"treasured people"—means that the Jewish people are not only dear to God but also protected and hidden from view.

The word *segula* appears four additional times in the Bible.

For the Lord has chosen Jacob for Himself, Israel for His special treasure. (Psalm 135:4).

I also gathered silver and gold for myself and the special treasures of kings and provinces. I acquired male and female singers, the delights of the sons of men, and musical instruments of all kinds. (Ecclesiastes 2:8).

Moreover, because I have set my affection on the house of my God, I have given to the house of my God, over and above all that I have prepared for the holy house, my own special treasure of gold and silver: (1 Chronicles 29:3)

"They shall be Mine," says the Lord of hosts, "For the day that I make a special treasure. And I will have compassion on them as a man has compassion on his own son who serves him." (Malachi 3:17).

Psalm 135 uses *segula* in the same manner as it is used in the Bible to describe the nation of Israel. In the verses from

Ecclesiastes and 1 Chronicles, *segula* refers to the wealth of kings, Solomon in Ecclesiastes and David in Chronicles. The fourth instance is interesting in that this is the only time *segula* appears to refer to something other than Israel or wealth. While most translators have *segula* referring to the nation of Israel here as well, this interpretation is not supported by the syntax of the verse. For example, here is this verse's New King James Bible translation.

"They shall be Mine," says the Lord of hosts, "On the day that I make them My special treasure. And I will spare them as a man spares his own son who serves him."

The inclusion of the word "them" is simply not what the verse says in Hebrew. The translators were likely basing themselves on the fact that in most other instances, *segula* does, in fact refer to Israel. But the simplest and most direct reading of the Hebrew is that *segula* refers to the day. For *segula* to refer to Israel here in Malachi, one must admit that a word is missing from the verse.

Simply put, the order of the words in the verse suggests that *segula* here refers to "the day", i.e., the redemption day itself. Rashi on Malachi comments:

For the day that I make a segula – that I have stored away and set aside to pay out my rewards. – (Rashi on Malachi 3:17).

Segula does not mean only a dear treasure that is guarded and stored away but one that is to be brought out into the open at some later date. The Talmud supports this meaning of segula.

If one has received funds that belong to a minor, he should make a segula for [the minor].(Talmud Bavli Bava Batra 52a).

The rule the Talmud describes pertains to an orphaned minor. If, due to either a lawsuit, an inheritance, or as a guardian, someone is holding or controlling funds belonging to the minor, he should not give the funds directly to the minor. Rather, he must set up a trust account. Later, when the minor reaches adulthood, they can access the funds. The sages of the Talmud used the word *segula* to describe the trust account.

If we combine all the above sources, we may suggest that the definition of *segula* is a treasure that is closely guarded against harm. It is concealed from view and saved until a later date in the future when it will be appropriate to bring it out into the open to realize its purpose.

The People of Israel are described as *am segula* – "a *segula* nation." Have these people been kept out of public view? We who have lived in the twentieth and twenty-first centuries might laugh at this notion. Jews are anything but out of view. However, for most of the history of the past two thousand years, Jews – the *am segula* – were very much hidden. General history books contain virtually nothing relating to the Jewish people during this period. Jews were a tiny, powerless minority who played almost no role in history. God stored us away, so to speak, protecting us and hiding us from the world. Over the past century or so, it is only recently that this *am segula* has been brought out of hiding and has assumed a most visible place on the world stage.

The answer to our question, "chosen for what?", can be summed up this way: The nation of Israel is precious to God. We were protected and hidden away until God chose to bring us out of hiding to fulfill our true purpose.

Perhaps this change is the beginning of the fulfillment of the verse in Malachi quoted above, which describes the ultimate redemption of Israel and the world.

For the day that I make a segula, I will have compassion on them as a man has compassion on a son who serves him.

May God bring the redemption speedily in our days.

Eikev

What is a Blessing?

THIS WEEK'S BIBLE portion contains the commandment to bless God after eating.

You will eat, be satisfied, and bless the Lord, your God, for the good land that He has given you. (Deuteronomy 8:10).

This blessing of God, known liturgically as *Birkat Hamazon* - Grace after meals, is one of the very few biblically mandated prayers. Almost all Jewish liturgy is rabbinic rather than biblical. But here, in an explicit verse in the Bible, we are commanded to bless God after we eat.

How are we to understand this obligation? The text explicitly instructs us to "bless" God after we eat. That is the verb that is used. But what exactly does it mean to "bless" God? When we say that someone is "blessed," we usually mean that the person in question has had something good bestowed upon them. Examples that come to mind are someone who is "blessed" with wealth or with a particular talent. Do we understand that when we bless God, we bestow something upon Him? The implication that there is some good that we could give God makes no sense. That God is complete and perfect is essential to His definition. To say that we could bestow anything upon Him implies that there is some way in which He could be improved. Furthermore, as God's creations, we cannot possibly possess anything to give God that does not come from Him to begin with. The inescapable conclusion is that when we talk about blessing God, we must refer to something other than the conventional use of the term.

Some might suggest that our thanks and appreciation are what we bestow upon God when we bless Him. I mentioned that Grace after Meals is biblically mandated by the verse quoted above. The problem with this simple explanation is that there is a word for thanks in Biblical Hebrew, but this verse does not use it. If the intent of the Bible were to command us to thank God for the food, a different verb would have been used. The text clearly tells us to "bless" God. Furthermore, within the Jewish traditional understanding of the verse going all the way back two thousand years, we see that this obligation to "bless" God after eating was not understood as simply thanking Him.

In the Talmud, the rabbinic requirement to recite a blessing of God before eating food is derived from the Biblical commandment to bless Him after eating.

The sages taught: What is the Bible source for Grace after Meals? [The Bible] states, 'You will eat, you will be satisfied, and you will bless the Lord, your God, for the good land that He has given you. (Deuteronomy. 8:10)' … This teaches us only [that we must bless] after eating. From where do we know [that we must bless] before eating? It is logical. If one must bless when one is satisfied [i.e. after eating], then when one is hungry, how much more so [must he bless]? (Talmud Bavli. Berachot 48b).

Here, the Talmud explains that blessing God when one is hungry makes more sense than when one is satisfied. Therefore, if the Bible requires a blessing after food, it is logical that a blessing is required before food. It seems from this Talmudic passage that the primary purpose of blessing God is not as an expression of thanks. If it were, the Talmud's logic would not make sense. Why would it make more sense to thank God when hungry than when satisfied?

Rashi's (11th century France) comment in the Talmud is as follows:

When he is hungry, and he is about to alleviate his hunger with the creation of the Holy One, Blessed is He, how much more so is he required to bless God even more? (Rashi, Talmud Berachot)

Obviously, a hungry person who is about to eat intends to alleviate his hunger with "God's creation." What else could he possibly eat? What is Rashi alluding to with this choice of words?

The Hebrew word for "blessing" is *beracha*. This word—or its verb root—first appears in the Bible on the fifth day of creation.

He blessed them [the fish], saying, 'Be fruitful and multiply and fill the water in the seas.' (Genesis 1:22).

Rashi comments:

AND HE BLESSED THEM — Because people decreased their number, hunting them and eating them, they needed a blessing (see Genesis Rabbah 11:2); it is true that beasts also were in need of a blessing, but on account of the serpent that was to be cursed in the future, He did not bless them, in order that it not be included in the blessing. (Rashi, Genesis. 1:22).

God told the fish that there would be many of them. In Biblical Hebrew, the word *beracha* – blessing – implies "abundance." God blessed the fish by saying, "May there be many of you." Blessing is the *realization of potential abundance*. Two fish or two people may have the potential to reproduce. This potential by itself is not, technically speaking, a "blessing." The "blessing" is realizing this potential when a child is produced. When we bless a friend, we are wishing upon them the realization of potential abundance in their lives.

When we "bless" God, we do not bestow anything on God. We are attempting to realize and actualize the world's hidden potential for abundant Godliness. When we say, "Blessed are You, our Lord…" we are saying to God, "Let there be more of you in the revealed reality of this world."

Let's sum up what we have said. Everything that God created can be used to reveal Him. Every one of God's creations contains latent Godliness. This Godliness exists in potential form. When we connect what we experience in the world to God, we are using His creation for its true purpose. We are using His creation to manifest His presence in the world. For example, if I take an apple and eat it without recognizing the Godliness within it – that it is one of God's creations – I have not revealed the potential Godliness in that apple. As a result, there is less awareness of God in the world. On the other hand, when I first recite a blessing and thus declare my recognition that this apple is an external manifestation of God, merely one small example of God's creation, I have actualized the potential of this apple to be a vehicle for the revelation of God in the world. Now, when I eat the apple, I no longer simply enjoy the flavor and nutrients. I am experiencing God. As a result of my blessing God, there is more God revealed in the world.

When blessings are recited, there is more perception of God

in the world. For this reason, there are blessings to be made on so many natural experiences. There is a blessing to say when one hears thunder when one sees blossoms in the spring, when a Bible commandment is performed, and even after going to the bathroom. Every experience in life is an experience of a particular aspect of God's world. When we say blessings over one of life's experiences – however great or small – we actualize the latent potential Godliness within that particular experience. We welcome God's presence into the world. In a revealed sense, there is *more* of Him. When we say, "Blessed are You, Lord," we are saying, "Dear God, we want Your presence to be revealed in abundance."

A famous Hassidic anecdote expresses this point. Reb Mendel of Kotzk's students asked him, "Rabbi, where is God?" Reb Mendel replied, "Wherever you let Him in."

Re'eih

Deuteronomy 11:26–16:17

Is Poverty Part of God's Plan?

A NUMBER OF VERSES in portion, Re'eih, address the topic of charity for the poor. The subject is mentioned in the context of a discussion of the forgiving of loans at the Sabbatical year. During the Sabbatical year, it is forbidden to farm the land every seventh year. Anything that grows on its own is free to be claimed by all. In addition to the forgiveness of debts, the fact that all produce in the land was freely available to all meant that the poor depended on the Sabbatical year for their livelihood. In this context, the Bible states:

> *However, may there be no needy person among you, as God will surely bless you in the land that God your Lord will give you as an inheritance to possess it? (Deuteronomy 15:4).*

Seven verses later, the Bible states:

> *For needy people will not cease to exist within the land; therefore, I command you, saying, 'You shall surely open your hand*

to your brother, to your poor, to your needy in your land.'
(Deuteronomy 15:11).

Many commentaries take note of the apparent contradiction between these two verses. Verse four states that God will bless us so that there will be no needy people in the land. Then, verse 11 states definitively that there will always be needy people. The Midrash (the ancient teachings of the Jewish sages from between the 1st and 4th centuries) responds to this problem with the following statement.

At a time when you are doing the will of the Omnipresent One, there are needy people among others and not among you. When you are not doing the will of the Omnipresent One, there are needy people among you. (Sifre 104, as quoted by Rashi).

The later commentaries explain the words of this teaching as follows. If the people of Israel followed all of God's commandments, there would be no poverty. As Nachmanides (13th century) puts it,

It is a promise that there will not be a needy person among [Israel] when they are keeping all the commandments. [God] said, 'But I know that not all the generations for all time will be entirely fulfilling the commandments, to the extent that it would not be needed to command [rules] for the needy at all. Nachmanides, Deuteronomy 15:11).

In other words, the first verse, promising no poverty in Israel, refers to the ideal situation in which all the commandments are being kept, and God has removed poverty from the land. The second verse, guaranteeing there will always be needy people, refers to those times in history when the generation is not keeping all of the commandments, and there is poverty.

This approach paints a picture of an ideal world in which there is no poverty at all. Let's imagine such a world. Is a world without poverty truly ideal? If there were no poverty, could there possibly be charity? If there is no one who is needy, there is no opportunity to give charity. This may seem to be a strange concern. Obviously, we would all be happy in a world without poverty. However, in certain critical ways, society would certainly suffer if there were no opportunities for charity.

Rabbi Moshe Shick (Hungary, 19th cent.) sees the second verse – the promise that there will always be needy people – as part of God's ideal.

> *[God] planted people in his world; some are rich, and some are poor for the good of humanity. If all were rich, there would be no relationships between people and money would be meaningless. Money is merely a tool for the fulfillment of His will, and if all [people] were equal, money could never be elevated [to a higher purpose].Maharam Shick al haBible Deuteronomy 11).*

Seen this way, the fact that some are needy serves a higher purpose. God guarantees that there will always be some needy among us in order to facilitate charitable interactions between people. One may imagine a similar argument for the value of illness as a guarantee that people will continue to visit the sick and pray for them. This approach, while interesting, is admittedly fraught with theological difficulty. Are all the evils of the world to be celebrated as allowing for acts of kindness and heroism? Furthermore, Rabbi Shick's approach does not help explain the meaning of the first verse, which promises no poverty.

Like Rabbi Shick, Rabbi Samson Raphael Hirsch (Germany, 19th cent.) sees poverty as a necessity.

It lies quite in the course of the natural development of things that — left to itself — the greatest difference in fortunes, want, and surplus. Poverty and riches should exist next to one another. The inequality of mental gifts would already produce such inequalities as a natural consequence, and two sons starting from home with exactly equal means, and one having to provide for a single child, the other for a large family would soon present a very considerable difference in their means... But this condition of need which naturally exists elsewhere in the world, you are not allowed to occur in your land, in the land of God's Bible.... under the regime of a Bible community, penury and need would only temporarily affect any individual, and with God's assistance, be changed to a happy existence on earth commensurate with the dignity of a human being. (S.R. Hirsch on Bible Deuteronomy 15:11).

As Rabbi Hirsch sees it, economic inequality and poverty are inevitable natural world features. They are the direct result of other imbalances and differences in people's aspirations and circumstances. The goal of the Bible is not equality of economic status. Rather, the goal is to limit the inevitable poverty to a minimum. According to Rabbi Hirsch, the meaning of the Midrashic quote above is that "when you are doing the will of the Omnipresent One" refers to caring for the needy. In other words, as long as the people do God's will and care for the poor, there will be no needy people. If we do not do God's will – we don't care for the poor – there will be poor people.

Rabbi Hirsch agrees with Rabbi Shick that poverty has value inasmuch as it facilitates charity. He sees the first verse—the one that promises an end to poverty—as a charge to the people to do something about it rather than as an actual promise that there will be no poverty.

If we accept the approach that poverty serves the higher purpose of creating the context for acts of charity, we must be careful not to undermine charity in other ways. As Rabbi Hirsch puts it,

> *The notice affixed to houses 'no beggars need apply, the owners subscribe generously to the public funds' has not engendered the Jewish spirit that this law has nourished. (S. R. Hirsch Deuteronomy 15:7).*

Rabbi Hirsch is teaching us an important lesson relevant to modern times when government programs have replaced much of the care for the needy that once fell on community members. If we start to think of the needy as the government's problem and content ourselves with the knowledge that our tax dollars help the poor, we may find ourselves falling out of the habit of charitable giving. This is one built-in problem with government programs to alleviate poverty. As Rabbis Shick Rav Hirsch points out, preserving this habit of giving may very well be why God allows poverty to exist at all.

Shoftim

Deuteronomy 16:18–21:9

Why is the Rabbinic Law Legitimate?

WHAT IS THE basis for rabbinic law? For many Bible-believing people outside of Judaism, the system of rabbinic Jewish practice appears to stray far from the instructions of the Bible. For Christians, this perception is amplified based on a number of verses in the New Testament portraying rabbinic law as "doctrines of men" (see Mark 7:7, Matthew 15:9). Many Christians see the adherence to laws that are not stated explicitly in Scripture as practice that is unbiblical. So, the question remains: where does the legitimacy of the rabbinic law come from?

Shoftim is a portion of the Bible that contains one of the key verses, if not the key verse, that provides the basis for the obligation to listen to the rulings and interpretations of the rabbis.

> *According to the instruction which they instruct you, according to the judgment which they tell you, you shall do; you shall not turn aside from that which they tell you, to the right or to the left. (Deuteronomy 17:11).*

The word for "instruction" is *Torah*. *Torah* is often translated as law. The root of *Torah* is identical to that of the word translated as "instruct" just two words later. It is the same as the root for "teacher" – *moreh*. But many Christian translations have this word as "sentence" (KJV, NKJV), implying that the meaning of the verse is not a requirement to obey laws enacted by the rabbis but is limited to acceptance of the ruling in a court case. This interpretation is based on the context of the verse.

> *If a matter of judgment will be obscure (beyond) for you, between blood and blood, between judgment and judgment, or between blemish and blemish, matters of dispute within your gates, then you shall arise and go up to the place which the Lord your God chooses. 9 And you shall come to the priests, the Levites, and to the judge there in those days, and inquire of them; they shall tell you the statement of judgment. 10 You shall do according to the statement which they pronounce upon you in that place which the Lord chooses. And you shall be careful to do according to all that they instruct you. 11 According to the instruction which they instruct you, according to the judgment which they tell you, you shall do; you shall not turn aside from that which they tell you, to the right or to the left. (Deuteronomy 17:8-11).*

(The Hebrew word for "blemish" here is *nega*, referring to leprous spots that must be evaluated by a Kohen-priest. As recorded in Leviticus 13-14, these blemishes needed to be assessed by a priest to determine their status as pure or impure. This explains the instruction to go to "the priests, the Levites" in addition to "the judge.")

Because this passage can be understood as referring to specific cases that are brought before the court, the aforementioned

Christian translations read verse 11 as mandating acceptance of the sentence in a specific case rather than as a blanket requirement to adhere to all legislation and instruction of rabbinic authority.

The problem with this understanding is twofold. First, if this were the meaning of the verse, it would render it redundant. The previous verse, verse 10, already stated:

> *You shall do according to the statement they pronounce upon you in the place the Lord chooses. And you shall be careful to do according to all that they instruct you.*

"The statement which they pronounce upon you" sounds like a requirement to follow the ruling in an isolated case. What is then added by the following verse? We have already been told to listen to the verdict. The next verse must be teaching us something else. The second issue is that the word *Torah* does not mean "verdict" or "sentence." It is never used this way.

But why is it so important to listen to the rabbis? Why is there such an obligation at all? Why not simply allow each person to read the word of God and interpret it to the best of their own ability? What is wrong with different interpretations? I'd like to offer two answers.

Consider the following law:

> *Work shall be done for six days, but the seventh day shall be a holy day for you, a Sabbath of rest to the Lord. Whoever does any work on it shall be put to death. (Exodus 35:2).*

The Bible mandates the death penalty for anyone who does any work on the Sabbath day. But what is the definition of work? To say that the interpretation of the law is up to each individual renders this law impossible to follow. Leaving aside the matter of the death penalty for Sabbath violators, something that is alien to our modern way of thinking, how would this ever be implemented?

Imagine someone brought before the court for "working" on the Sabbath day. For example, this person was witnessed moving furniture in preparation for a large Sabbath meal. Is that "work"? Or someone mowing their lawn, doing their taxes, or discussing a business deal. It's one thing to say that each person has his own definition of "work." But the Bible mandates a death penalty to be implemented by the court for such a violation. How could any case ever be adjudicated? Clearly, to have a death penalty for work on the Sabbath day, there must be a universally agreed upon and legislated definition of "work." And if we have agreed upon definitions of work that are legally binding on everyone, *voila!* we have now accepted the authority of rabbinic interpretation.

This is merely one example of a larger point. The Bible is written to assume that there will be an authoritative body that interprets and implements the laws. There is no way around this.

The second answer is that the Bible itself prophecies that the people of Israel will spend many generations in exile. This means two things. First, the nation will be scattered and separated from each other for a long time. Without a unified interpretation of the law, it would have been a certainty that the Jewish people would, over the passage of the centuries, have become separate peoples and separate religions. The glue that kept the Jewish people together during the exile is the adherence to the same set of laws, the rabbinic law.

Second, during the centuries of exile, the practice of Bible law built around the Temple, the sacrifices, and many of the other laws that are only applicable in the land of Israel were impossible to keep. Without rabbinic laws mandating all manner of worship and ritual observance beyond what is written in the

Bible, there would be no way for the Jewish people to maintain any kind of cohesive religious identity.

Simply put, the Jewish people would not have survived the exile without their steadfast commitment to rabbinic law. Rather than being a burden, as Christians often portray it, rabbinic law is critical to God's plan for Israel's survival and flourishing.

Ki Teitzei

Deuteronomy 21:10–25:19

Destroying Amalek: Timing is Everything

T HE CLOSING LINES of the Bible portion Ki Teitzei deal with
an old foe of the People of Israel: Amalek.

> *Remember what Amalek perpetrated against you on the way*
> *when you were going out of Egypt. When they chanced upon*
> *you en route struck down your tail – those straggling behind*
> *you – and you were exhausted and wearied, and they had*
> *no fear of God. When the Lord your God has given you rest*
> *from all your enemies around, in the land that the Lord your*
> *God is giving you to inherit, you shall obliterate the memory*
> *of Amalek from beneath the heavens; do not forget. (Deuter-*
> *onomy 25:17-19).*

Two commandments are stated in this passage. The first commandment is always to remember what Amalek did, as the passage begins by commanding us to "remember" and ends with
the words, "Do not forget." The second direct commandment
is to "obliterate the memory of Amalek from beneath the sky."

This second obligation – to wipe out Amalek – is introduced with a caveat that is unique among all the commandments in the Torah:

"When the Lord your God has given you rest from all your enemies around, in the land that the Lord your God is giving you to inherit."

From a simple reading, it appears that this is a *prerequisite* for the commandment to "obliterate the memory of Amalek." It is not unusual for commandments in the Torah to have clearly stated prerequisite times or places. For example, there are many commandments that apply only in the land of Israel. These are often introduced with the words, "When you will enter into the land…" But this prerequisite is unique. Apparently, the commandment to destroy Amalek applies only when the nation of Israel is perfectly secure on its land and has no active enemies that threaten it.

The great medieval commentator Rabbi Abraham Ibn Ezra (12th cent. Spain) addresses this point:

This commandment applies after they inherit the land, and the land will be silent from war all around its borders for as long as they are involved in the wars that they have in the near future [i.e., the wars to conquer the land]. They are not obligated to make war with Amalek. (Ibn Ezra, Deuteronomy. 25:19).

According to Ibn Ezra, there is no prohibition against destroying Amalek before the time of national security and quiet. The destruction of Amalek is always *permitted*. However, it is only an *obligation* to do so once Israel is safe from all surrounding enemies. Ibn Ezra understands the caveat "When the Lord has given you rest..." not as a prerequisite for any fulfillment of the commandment but as a condition for the obligatory, rather than optional, nature of the commandment. But the plain meaning of the verse can just as easily be understood as *prohibiting* the obliteration of Amalek before the stated conditions of tranquility are met.

In almost all cases, the purpose of war is either to capture land or to defend against attack or imminent threat. The latter may involve a pre-emptive strike to ensure victory. But in the case of this command to make war with Amalek, security is not the issue. The Torah commands a war on Amalek only when the security concerns of Israel are non-existent. The purpose of this battle is neither national defense nor the capture of land.

This unique feature of the obligation to destroy Amalek – that it only applies when Israel is completely secure – contains a powerful lesson.

Amalek is not an ordinary enemy of the People of Israel. Amalek is Israel's archenemy because Amalek's attack in Exodus 17 was the prototype of audacity in the face of God. God had just taken Israel out of Egypt. The ten miraculous plagues were an explicit demonstration of the hand of God. God then split the sea and drowned the Egyptians in it. Almost immediately following this, Amalek attacked. One has to wonder what Amalek was thinking. Did they really think that they had a chance of victory over Israel after what God had just done to Egypt? The answer is that Amalek believed in chance and coincidence. They believed that while there is a God, God's will is random and subject to change. The fact that God saved Israel on one day says nothing about what will happen on the next. The possibility that God directs the course of the history of a specific people to bring holiness into the world was repugnant to Amalek.

To put this another way, the only way to explain the seemingly irrational audacity of Amalek in attacking Israel immediately after the Exodus is to conclude that they did not believe that God had any special providential relationship with Israel. And this is what makes Amalek Israel's archenemy.

One of the primary purposes of Israel, if not *the* primary purpose, is to be a vehicle for the revelation of God in this world. God reveals Himself through Israel by directing their history in miraculous ways. The Egyptians who witnessed the ten plagues recognized God through His redemption of Israel. Similarly, in our time, the unprecedented, biblically foretold, miraculous return of the nation of Israel to their land testifies to God's control over history. To believe that God has no special concern for Israel and that whatever happens in history is due to human action and change is the essence of Amalek. As our passage puts it, "they had no fear of God."

If Israel wages war to destroy Amalek at a time when Israel still has security concerns, the true purpose of the war would not be clear. Under such circumstances, most people would see the goal of this war as ensuring Israel's safety from a bitter foe. The motive for going to war would not be the destruction of evil. Such a war would be understood as having a political rather than spiritual purpose. However, at a time when Israel is safe and secure, there is no political need for a war. In such a situation, the purpose of a war with Amalek is clear to all. With no political or security need, the only reason for such a war is the destruction of evil.

One might ask, at a time when Israel has achieved total peace and security and has no threat from any direction, why should we attack Amalek altogether? Perhaps the purpose of the attack is to remove any future threat from Amalek. However, this is not the case. Amalek is to be attacked even if they pose no threat of any kind to Israel. Destroying Amalek is a value unto itself.

It is interesting to note that Amalek was criticized for attacking Israel with nothing to gain and without provocation. Israel was not near Amalek's borders when they attacked. It is an interesting quid pro quo that their fate is to be attacked at a time when there is no practical benefit to Israel in doing so.

As mentioned above, Amalek represents the ideological opposite of the Torah and Israel. This means that when Israel fully follows the Torah and God's will, it represents the opposite of Amalek. When Israel does not follow God's Torah, then Amalek and Israel cease to be opposites.

The war on Amalek must be clearly understood as the triumph of those who believe in God's mastery of world events over those who deny it. And this clarity is only possible when Israel is living in obedience to God. Moses told Israel numerous times that the ultimate reward for faithfully adhering to the will of God is that Israel will dwell securely in their land. In other words, "When the Lord your God has given you rest from all your enemies around, in the land that the Lord your God is giving you to inherit," is a time of optimal obedience to the word of God. This is the ideal context for the defeat of Amalek. Only then is the war against Amalek a war that is truly on behalf of God. As Moses said back in Exodus at the time of the original attack:

And Moses built an altar and called it The Lord Is My Banner, saying, "A hand upon the throne of the Lord! The Lord will have war with Amalek from generation to generation." (Exodus 17:15-16).

Ki Tavo
Deuteronomy 21:10–25:19

The Perils of Being a Parable

Towards the end of the portion, Ki Tavo, we find one of the darkest passages in the entire Bible. Fifty-four consecutive verses detail the harsh punishments that will befall the people of Israel should they turn their backs on God in disobedience. Plague, famine, defeat in war, exile, and all manner of suffering are listed (Deuteronomy 28:15-69). Among the many frightening and disturbing punishments, there is one that is difficult to understand.

> *You will be a source of astonishment, a proverb, and a conversation piece among all the people where God will lead you. (Deuteronomy 28:37).*

What does it mean to be "a proverb," a *mashal* in Hebrew? The great commentator Rashi (11th century France) comments:

> *A proverb: When a terrible affliction smites a person, they will say, 'This is like the affliction of so-and-so.'*

In other words, to be *a proverb* is to be a paradigm or figure of speech for the purpose of exaggeration. Our suffering will be so severe that it will become a metaphor, i.e., "Like the suffering of the Jews." Jewish suffering will become the paradigm for all suffering. We have seen an example of this in our day when it seems that every evil perpetrated on an ethnic group is compared to the Holocaust – often inappropriately due to exaggeration.

While this interpretation of the punishment fits with the plain meaning of the word *mashal* – "proverb," I find it unsatisfying for two reasons.

The first problem is that it is a strange punishment. After all, should we really care if other people use our suffering as a metaphor? It's true that it means that our suffering will be severe. On the other hand, if the suffering of the Jewish people becomes a common metaphor for suffering, this also means that the severity of our suffering will be well-known. This is not necessarily a bad thing. Furthermore, how is our suffering any worse due to other people using it as a proverb?

The second problem relates to context.

Here is our verse and the verse immediately preceding it.

The Lord will lead you and your king, whom you set over you, to a nation you know, neither you nor your fathers, and there you shall serve other gods, wood, and stone. You will be a source of astonishment, a proverb, and a conversation piece among all the peoples where God will lead you. (Deuteronomy 28:36-37).

Verse 36 is about going into exile. The punishment in our verse will happen "among all the peoples where God will lead you." Clearly, the punishment of becoming "a source of astonishment, a proverb, and a conversation piece" is connected to Israel's exile among the nations of the world. Why? We should note that most of the horrific punishments in the list are described as happening in the land of Israel. Why is this one becoming a metaphor for suffering, specifically linked to exile among the nations?

I'd like to suggest a different interpretation of this punishment to answer these questions.

The Hebrew word *mashal* implies not only a proverb in the sense mentioned above, i.e., a metaphor or figure of speech, but *Mashal* also means "parable." For example, in Ezekiel 17, God tells Ezekiel to "speak a parable to the House of Israel." (Ezekiel 17:2) What follows is a parable of two eagles and a vine (v. 3-10). After the conclusion of the parable, God tells Ezekiel that it is meant to convey the rebellion of King Zedekiah and the consequences that will follow. The word for "parable" in this passage in Ezekiel is *mashal.*

A parable is an allegorical story meant to teach a lesson. When we say that a story is a parable, we mean that it is not factually true—it didn't happen. It's a fable, a myth. I'd like to suggest that this also means mashal in Deuteronomy 28:37.

The Jewish people have a unique relationship to history. Most people in the world today – certainly in the modern Western world – do not see themselves as the direct descendants of any ancient people. For example, when people study the history of ancient Mesopotamia or the ancient Greeks, nobody alive today identifies with these people. When Italian children study the history of the Roman Empire, they don't identify it as their own personal story. While it is obvious that everyone in the world today is a descendant of somebody from the ancient world, most people do not think that way.

The Jewish people consider themselves direct descendants of an ancient people. We are aware that Abraham is our great-grandfather, our ancestors left Egypt, and David and Solomon were once our kings. More to the point, we know that Israel is our ancestral homeland, and we have always stated that as a clear and open fact.

The history of Jewish continuity is a matter of record. Other than a few very short gaps, there are continuous written records of Jewish communal life from every century and every generation of Jews going back 2000 years.

Despite the empirical evidence, there are many who claim that the Jewish people of today are not the same Jewish people from Biblical times. Beyond the question of historical evidence, most people today just do not take Jewish claims of continuity seriously. To illustrate the point, if a leader of the State of Israel were to point out in the international media that our claim to Israel is based on the fact that our grandparents were exiled by the Romans over 1900 years ago, how many skeptics would laugh at that claim? Jewish continuity over thousands of years does not seem realistic to people because they see no connection between themselves and their own ancestors from ancient times.

A few years ago, I was invited by a Presbyterian pastor from the United States to speak to her church after she had met me on a visit to Israel. As a member of the Presbyterian Church of the United States of America (PCUSA), she requested permission from the General Presbyter of her state to host the event. The PCUSA has had an obsessive antagonism to Israel for many years. For example, at their 2018 General Assembly, they passed resolutions referring to Israel as "a colonial project" and as "an apartheid state". Just Googling "PCUSA and Israel" will provide easy access to these and other similar positions.

The General Presbyter's response was lukewarm. Unsurprisingly, he was not happy with her request. However, a particular statement in his email response to the pastor caught me off guard.

"I don't think the Old Testament nation of Israel and the present-day nation of Israel are equivalent. Nor should they be in my estimation."

Think about that. This Presbyterian leader, certainly well-versed in the Bible, had no problem dismissing the record of Jewish continuity over thousands of years. For him and many others who think like him, the Exodus from Egypt, the Bible, and the People of Israel in Temple times are not the actual history of our people. They see Jewish history as a fable, "a parable."

This way of thinking about the Jews has its origins in the Christian tradition of allegorical interpretation of the Bible popularized by Origen in the 3rd Century. Once the stories and prophecies in the Bible are understood only as allegories, it is easy to dismiss Jewish identity as irrelevant. If the Biblical stories are not meant to be taken literally, there is really no legitimacy to any claim that the Jewish people today are the same people described as Israel in the Bible.

Now we can understand why the Bible states that this punishment only occurs in exile. Had we never gone into exile, would anyone doubt our claims to the land? Would anyone brazenly assert that the Jewish people of today are not the same as Biblical Israel? The very fact of the exile and dispersion made possible the false perception that we lack a genealogical connection to ancient Israel.

And this is a terrible punishment. When the nations of the world dismiss Jewish history as a quaint fable, the Jewish people cease to have a legitimate identity. This is the meaning of the words, "You shall be a parable."

Nitzavim

Deuteronomy 29:9-30:20

The Unintended Irony of Replacement Theology

D EUTERONOMY 30 IS one of the most remarkable passages in the entire Bible. To help us appreciate Moses's extraordinary prophecy, let's review the chapters leading up to it.

In Deuteronomy 28, Moses related the blessings for obedience and punishments for disobedience of God's law to the people of Israel. Near the end of the chapter, we see that exile and dispersion are the ultimate punishment for disobedience.

> *Then the Lord will scatter you among all peoples, from one end of the earth to the other, and there you shall serve other gods, which neither you nor your fathers have known — wood and stone. – (Deuteronomy 28:64).*

Then, in chapter 29, Moses continues by telling the nation that the land will lie desolate while they are in exile. Moses even describes how in the future, people from other nations will see the destruction of the land and the exile of the Jewish people and conclude that God has done this because the Jews turned their backs on God. (Deuteronomy 29:22-28).

There will be more on that later. Then comes Deuteronomy 30. Here, Moses tells the people that after many generations of dispersion to the earth's four corners, they will return to the land.

> *The Lord your God will bring you back from captivity, and have compassion on you, and gather you again from all the nations where the Lord your God has scattered you. If any of you are driven out to the farthest parts under heaven, from there, the Lord your God will gather you, and from there, He will bring you. Then the Lord your God will bring you to the land which your fathers possessed, and you shall possess it. He will prosper you and multiply you more than your fathers. (Deuteronomy 30:3-5)*

The modern state of Israel today is populated by millions of Jews from every corner of the earth. The Jewish people have returned en masse to our land. We have taken possession of it in the form of Jewish sovereignty. Israel is a prosperous nation. And there are more Jews in the land today than at any other time in history. Every detail of this biblical prophecy, spoken over 3300 years ago, has been fulfilled in our time. Since it was uttered, everyone who read the Bible saw these verses as a future prophecy. But today, we live in a time when every word of these verses is a reality.

However, not all who profess belief in the Bible see these verses this way. For most of the past 2000 years, the standard doctrine of Christianity regarding the Jews was what is known as *Supersessionism* or *Replacement Theology*. This is the belief that the church had replaced Israel.

According to Supersessionism, the Jewish people were originally the chosen people in covenant with God. However, due to their disobedience and violation of the covenant, the Jews lost this status. The covenant of Israel was transferred to the church. For those who adhere to this belief today, the modern state of Israel is not a fulfillment of Deuteronomy 30. When they look at the millions of Jews from all corners of the earth who populate the land of Israel under Jewish sovereignty, they do not see Biblical prophecy fulfilled.

But here's the irony: their denial that the modern state of Israel is a fulfillment of these prophecies is included in the prophecies themselves!

Just a few verses before the Deuteronomy 30 prophecy we quoted, the Bible says:

> *It will be said by the coming generation of your children who rise up after you, and the foreigner who comes from a far land, when they see the plagues of that land and the sicknesses which the Lord has laid on it, 'The whole land is brimstone, salt, and burning; it cannot be sown, it cannot sprout, nor can any grass grow in it, like the overthrow of Sodom and Gomorrah, Admah, and Zeboiim, which the Lord overthrew in His anger and His wrath.' All nations will say, 'Why has the Lord done so to this land? What does this furious anger mean?' Then people would say: 'Because they have forsaken the covenant of the Lord God of their fathers, which He made with them when He brought them out of the land of Egypt; for they went and served other gods and worshiped them, gods, that they did not know and that He had not given to them. Then the anger of the Lord was aroused against this land to bring on it every curse that is written in this book. And the Lord uprooted them from their land in anger, in wrath, and in great indignation, and cast them into another land, as it is this day.' "The secret things belong to the Lord our God,*

but those things which are revealed belong to us and to our
children forever, that we may do all the words of this law.
(Deuteronomy 29:21-28).

Here, Moses foretells a time when the nations will look at
the Jews' exile and the desolation of the land of Israel and conclude that the covenant between Israel and God has ended. It's
worth noting that the nations in this passage are familiar with
the Bible. The text explicitly states that they will compare the
land of Israel to the cities that God overturned in Genesis 19.
Furthermore, these people are clearly aware of "every curse that
is *written in this book.*"

Incredibly, Moses described people from the nations of the
world who know and believe in the Bible but also believe that
God's covenant with the Jewish people has ended. Imagine hearing this prophecy when Moses originally spoke it over 3300 years
ago. This detail would seem absurd. Why would there be nations
who profess belief in the Bible but believe that God has broken
His covenant with the Jewish people? Without the founding
and spread of Christianity, who among the nations of the world
would even know the Bible?

Christian theologians who promoted Replacement Theology
looked at the Jews' seemingly endless exile and the desolation
of the land and came to the exact conclusion foretold by Moses
in these verses. From the reality that they saw before them, it
appeared that God had revoked the covenant from the Jewish
people. Ironically, these theologians were fulfilling this prophecy
by espousing their erroneous doctrine without even realizing it!

So why did they make this mistake? The answer is right here
in the text as well. Immediately after this prediction of Supersessionism, Moses tells us, "The secret things belong to the Lord."
In other words, don't think you can look at reality and come to

your own conclusions about God based on what you see. Even if, in your time, it looks to you like God has given up on Israel, don't draw your own conclusions about God's plans. Read the Bible. The covenant is forever.

Vayeilech

Deuteronomy 31:1-30

The Strange Prediction of Israel's Sinful Future

I N DEUTERONOMY 31, we read about the transition of leadership from Moses to his successor and student, Joshua. First, Moses, on his own initiative, called Joshua forward:

> *Then Moses called Joshua and said to him in the sight of all Israel, "Be strong and of good courage, for you must go with this people to the land which the Lord has sworn to their fathers to give them, and you shall cause them to inherit it. And the Lord, He is the One who goes before you. He will be with you, He will not leave you nor forsake you; do not fear nor be dismayed." (Deuteronomy 31:7-8).*

Moses made a public display of appointing Joshua and reminding him and all present that God would be with Joshua. Then, a few verses later, we read:

> *Then the Lord said to Moses, "Behold, the days approach when you must die; call Joshua, and present yourselves in the tent of*

meeting, that I may commission him." So Moses and Joshua went and presented themselves in the tent of meeting. And the Lord appeared at the tent in a pillar of cloud, and the pillar of cloud stood above the door of the tent. (ibid v.14-15).

At this point, we would expect the next verses to show God commissioning Joshua to succeed Moses. But that is not what we find at all. Instead, the following passage appears:

And the Lord said to Moses: "Behold, you will lie down with your fathers; and this people will rise and play the harlot with the gods of the foreigners of the land, where they go to be among them, and they will forsake Me and break My covenant which I have made with them. Then My anger shall be aroused against them in that day, and I will forsake them, and I will hide My face from them, and they shall be devoured. And many evils and troubles shall befall them, so that they will say in that day, 'Have not these evils come upon us because our God is not among us?' And I will surely hide My face that day because of all the evil they have done, in that they have turned to other gods. "Now therefore, write down this song for yourselves, and teach it to the children of Israel; put it in their mouths, that this song may be a witness for Me against the children of Israel. When I have brought them to the land flowing with milk and honey, of which I swore to their fathers, and they have eaten and filled themselves and grown fat, they will turn to other gods and serve them, provoke Me, and break My covenant. Then it shall be when many evils and troubles have come upon them, that this song will testify against them as a witness; for it will not be forgotten in the mouths of their descendants, for I know the inclination of their behavior today, even before I have brought them to the land of which I swore to give them."

Moses wrote this song the same day and taught it to the children of Israel (ibid, v.16-22).

And then, in verse 23, we finally find God commissioning Joshua to be Moses' successor.

Then He inaugurated Joshua, the son of Nun, and said, "Be strong and of good courage; for you shall bring the children of Israel into the land of which I swore to them, and I will be with you."(v. 23).

This is strange. This verse should have come immediately after verse 15. Why did God interrupt the call for Joshua to come forward to be commissioned by Him with this lengthy message to Moses about the certainty of the children of Israel sinning after his death?

It is worth noting that a few chapters ago, in Deuteronomy 28, we read an extensive list of punishments that would befall the nation of Israel in the future if and when they would sin and stray from God. What is the purpose of this passage here? Why did God choose this moment to tell Moses that the people would certainly sin after his death? What is God's point?

Let's ask one more question about the sequence of this chapter. After verse 23, where God commissioned Joshua, Moses then told the leaders of Israel what God had told him just before.

"for I know your rebellion and your stiff neck. If today, while I am yet alive with you, you have been rebellious against the Lord, then how much more after my death? Gather to me all the elders of your tribes and your officers, that I may speak these words in their hearing and call heaven and earth to witness against them. For I know that after my death, you will

become utterly corrupt and turn aside from the way which I have commanded you. And evil will befall you in the latter days because you will do evil in the sight of the Lord, to provoke Him to anger through the work of your hands." (v. 27-29

Why did Moses do this? It's one thing to warn people not to sin, but that's not what he's doing here. Moses told the leadership of Israel that they would certainly "become utterly corrupt" after his death. What kind of parting message is this as he passes the baton of leadership?

I'd like to suggest that this prophetic message, that the nation would certainly become more sinful and corrupt after Moses' death, was critical to the success of Joshua's leadership going forward. Allow me to explain.

Imagine that this negative message was not delivered. Imagine that the transition of leadership from Moses to Joshua, including God commissioning Joshua in front of the entire people, had happened without this pessimistic prediction. What would have happened when, under Joshua's leadership, the people would begin to stray from God? What would the reaction of the people be if they felt the nation slipping away from the lofty spiritual level they had been on during the time of Moses?

They would question their leader. Inevitably, the people would attribute the decline in national piety to Joshua's ineffectiveness. They would wonder if Joshua was the wrong person for the job. Losing faith in Joshua's leadership would have disastrous consequences.

Telling the people in advance that they would undoubtedly stray from God after Moses' death, ironically, minimized the damage this straying would cause in terms of national cohesion. Now, when the spiritual backsliding takes place, nobody will think of blaming Joshua. After all, God and Moses had already said that this would happen. Everyone would understand that it had nothing to do with any deficiency in Joshua. This way, despite the problems that straying from God obviously brings, a lack of faith in Joshua's leadership would not be one of them.

Now we understand the strange sequence of verses in chapter 31. God inserted the prediction of the spiritual backsliding into a scene of the commissioning of Joshua because the purpose of this prediction was to reinforce trust in Joshua as the leader of Israel.

Ha'azinu

Deuteronomy 32:1-52

Seeing God in the Study of History

ALMOST THE ENTIRETY of the portion, Haazinu is a poem in which Moses speaks to the nation of Israel in the final days of his life. Opening with the words, "Give ear, O heavens, and I will speak; And hear O earth, the words of my mouth" (Deuteronomy 32:1), Moses lays out his goal in composing this poem.

> *As I proclaim the name of the Lord, ascribe greatness to our God. The Rock, His work is perfect; for all His ways are justice, a God of truth and without injustice; righteous and upright is He. (Deuteronomy 32:3-4).*

Moses tells us that the purpose of these verses is to show that God is perfect, righteous, and just in all His ways. This is no small issue. After the preceding chapters described in great detail the suffering and exile that would befall the people of Israel in the future, the topic of Divine Justice is certainly relevant in context. But Moses does not merely declare that God is perfect, just, etc. In this poem, He gives us a roadmap to understand and experience God's righteousness.

Beginning in verse 8, the thirty-six verses that follow tell the story of history. To sum up:

- God separated the world into nations and peoples (v. 8)
- He chose the children of Israel and looked after them with special miraculous providence (v. 9-14)
- Israel rebelled against God (v. 16-18)
- God responds with fury, punishment, and exile (v. 19-26)
- God withholds destroying Israel because Israel's enemies are arrogant and faithless (v. 27-33)
- God vows to take vengeance on the enemies of Israel for their excess cruelty and lack of faith (v. 34-36)
- False beliefs will be proven wrong (v. 37-39)
- God enacts vengeance and judgment on the enemies of Israel (v. 40-42)
- In God's punishment of the nations, He avenges the evils done to Israel, bringing atonement for His land and His people (v.42)

It is important to note that nowhere in this poem do we find the people of Israel repenting of their sins. God does not avenge the cruel treatment of the Jews because the Jews have earned it. In this narrative of history, God punishes the evil enemies of Israel to protect His own honor, not for the sake of Israel.

Considering this last point, that God's redemption of Israel and His punishment of the nations are not dependent on any repentance by the Jewish people, we must ask a basic question about this entire chapter. What exactly is the lesson that Moses was trying to teach?

I'd like to suggest that Moses states the message of this entire poem in the verse just before the narrative begins in verse 8.

Recall the days of yore and examine the years of each generation. Ask your father and he will tell you, your elders, and they will speak to you. (Deuteronomy 32:7).

In other words, Moses commands us to study history. The Hebrew word *olam* is translated here as "yore." Many other translations have "Remember the days of old." Both "yore" and "old" imply only looking back at the past. But *olam* does not have any past-tense connotation. Olam appears over 400 times in the Bible. While there are a few verses in which *olam* refers to the past, most of the time, *olam* is used it refer to the future, best translated as "eternity." For example:

The rainbow shall be in the cloud, and I will look on it to remember the everlasting covenant between God and every living creature of all flesh that is on the earth. (Genesis 9:16).

For all the land which you see, I give to you and your descendants forever (Genesis 13:15).

Olam does not mean "the past." Neither does it mean "the future." Rather, *Olam* is the totality of time, and *eternity*. So in this verse here in Deuteronomy, Moses tells us to "Recall the days of *olam*." In other words, we must look at the events of the world through the widest possible lens. We must look at the totality of history.

As I quoted at the beginning of this teaching, Moses opened by declaring that all God's ways are perfect, just, and righteous. He then instructed us to study the full scope of history. These two ideas are inextricably linked. If we look at events of history through a narrow lens, we will misunderstand what is happening. Injustice will be more apparent if we don't take the long view.

Individual events, even specific eras, can easily give the impression of terrible injustices in God's running of the world. Only when the fullest sweep of history is considered can we clearly see what God is doing. Only then can we see the justice of God's ways.

In his poem, Moses tells us that the entire arc of history has one purpose: to reveal God to the world. All nations, all events, all the ups and downs in the story of Israel, everything is part of a single narrative. This perspective is not natural to us as human beings living in the present.

Imagine you are flipping channels and happen in the middle of a movie. You watch a few scenes. There's an argument, a car chase, a fistfight. Then, you flip away to another channel. What happened in the movie? Who was the good guy? Who was the bad guy? Was justice served? Drawing conclusions from a few scenes in the middle is a recipe for misunderstanding. The same is true with us in our lives here on God's earth. Our lives are fleeting moments in the great story of history. To expect to see divine justice work itself out during our short lifetimes is unrealistic and impossible.

Here, near the end of his life, Moses tells us how we can begin to understand God.

"Recall the days of eternity, examine the years of each generation. Ask your father, and he will tell you, your elders, and they will speak to you. (Deuteronomy 32:7).

Widen your lens. Study the entire story, beginning with Adam, Abraham, and Moses and ending with the future as described in the Bible. Examine the generations. Seek the wisdom and perspective of those who came before you. This is how we see God in History.

Vezot Haberacha

Deuteronomy 33:1-34:12

Moses' Hidden Grave

Mose, the servant of the Lord, died there in the land of Moab, according to the word of the Lord. And He buried him in the valley in the land of Moab, opposite Beth Peor; but no one knows his grave to this day. (Deuteronomy 34:5-6).

IN THE CLOSING verses of the Bible, we read of Moses's death. The Bible testifies that Moses was buried by none other than God Himself. As for the location of Moses's grave, the Bible tells us that "no one knows his grave to this day." In fact, Moses's gravesite remains unknown. This leads to the obvious question: Why was it necessary to conceal Moses's gravesite?

What's even more puzzling is that immediately before telling us that "no one knows his grave," the verse records the precise location. It should be noted that most stories in the Bible do not include precise locations. We are usually told about the general area where events take place. The amount of detail regarding the burial place of Moses is unusual. "In the valley in the land of Moab, opposite Beth Peor." It almost seems as though the text of the Bible is taunting us. After all, what is the point of recording such a detailed description of the location only to then state that nobody can find it?

In the Talmud, the Jewish sages addressed this difficulty with a story. We should note that the stories in the Talmud are not necessarily meant to be taken literally as historical accounts. The sages often used stories and parables to convey theological ideas, as was common in ancient times.

> *"And He buried him in the valley in the land of Moab over against Beth Peor, and no man knows of his grave to this day" (Deuteronomy 34:6). Rabbi Berekhya says: This verse provides a marker within a marker (i.e., a very precise description of the location of his burial) and yet "no man knows of his grave to this day"? The evil kingdom (the Roman Empire) once sent messengers to the garrison of Beth Peor and said to them: 'Show us where Moses is buried.' As the men stood above on the upper section of the mountain, it appeared to them as if the grave was below in the lower section. As they stood below, it appeared to them to be above. They divided into two groups, one above and one below. To those who were standing above, the grave appeared to them to be below; to those who were standing below, the grave appeared to them to be above, to fulfill that which is stated: "And no man knows of his grave to this day" (Deuteronomy 34:6). – Talmud Sotah 13b-14a.*

The premise of the story is simple enough. The Romans, who ruled the land of Israel and the surrounding area, decided to find Moses' burial place based on the location described in our verse. They went to the valley in the land of Moab opposite Beth Peor, but they could not find the grave. The story ends by stating that the inability of the Roman garrison to locate Moses' gravesite was a fulfillment of the verse that states that "no man knows of his grave to this day." Which leaves us with our original question. Why did God choose to conceal Moses' grave?

Moses played a unique role in the story of Israel. The Bible itself attests to his status as the greatest prophet of all time more than once.

Hear now My words: If there will be a prophet for you, I, the Lord, make Myself known to him in a vision; I speak to him in a dream. Not so with My servant Moses; He is trusted in all My house. Mouth to mouth, I speak with him in a vision that is not in riddles, and he gazes upon the image of the Lord. (Numbers 12:6-8).

There has not again arisen in Israel a prophet like Moses, whom the Lord knew face to face.(Deuteronomy 34:10).

While it is beyond us to fully comprehend the unique nature of the prophetic experience of Moses, we see clearly from these verses that God Himself declared that the prophecy of Moses was unlike that of any prophet before or since. More to the point, we are told that the word of God came to Moses more clearly and not in a vision. In other words, Moses was not shown a vision that he would then interpret and describe to others. This is the manner of prophecy of all other prophets. Moses was spoken to "mouth to mouth." God declared him to be "trusted in all My house."

In order to be sure that the law was transmitted with perfect accuracy, the prophecy of Moses needed to be different. The words of commanded law could not be Moses' own, based on the interpretation of a vision. He would need to transmit God's words exactly. This role of transmitter of the law began immediately after the Ten Commandments were spoken by God. Upon hearing God's voice the people were afraid and asked that Moses relay God's word instead.

Then they said to Moses, "You speak with us, and we will hear; but let not God speak with us, lest we die." (Exodus 20:19).

From that point forward, God told Moses the commandments, and he relayed them to the people. In other words, of the 613 commandments in the Bible, the people heard only the Ten Commandments from God. The rest were transmitted through Moses.

Besides transmitting God's law, Moses also served as an intermediary between the people and God when God was angered by the children of Israel. On several occasions during the time in the desert, Moses interceded and prayed to God on behalf of the people. Most notably, after the sin of the Golden Calf, Moses saved Israel from destruction.

Let's consider Moses' role from the perspective of the people of Israel. It was Moses who performed the plagues in Egypt, raised his staff to split the Red Sea, and relayed the word of God to the people. He spent forty days and forty nights on Mount Sinai without eating or drinking when he ascended to receive the Bible, an impossible feat for any normal person. He saved Israel from destruction with the strength of his prayers. We could go on, but you get the point.

To the children of Israel, Moses did not seem exactly human. We need to look no further than the sin of the Golden Calf.

Now, when the people saw that Moses delayed coming down

from the mountain, the people gathered around Aaron and said to him, "Come, make us gods that shall go before us; for as for this Moses, the man who brought us up out of the land of Egypt, we do not know what has become of him." (Exodus 32:1).

The sages meant this by the story from the Talmud about the Roman garrison that went to look for Moses' grave.

To those who were standing above, the grave appeared to them to be below; to those who were standing below, the grave appeared to them to be above,

To look at Moses as a normal human, he appeared as a higher being. But to look at him as a god, he appeared human.

I'd like to suggest that it is due to Moses' unique status that his grave needed to be concealed. The temptation to view Moses as a god-like figure was great. Seeing him as an intermediary who could intercede with God on our behalf was certainly tempting. It is not difficult to imagine that had the location of Moses' gravesite been known, it would certainly have become a pilgrimage site. People would flock there to pray… to Moses instead of God.

God sent us an important message by concealing Moses' gravesite. The Bible makes this lesson clear by including the precise location of Moses' grave in the verse. We can't find Moses' grave because God has ordained that we will not find it, not because we don't know where he was buried. To prove the point, the Bible tells us exactly where it is.

Yes, Moses did in fact serve as an intermediary. This role was necessary for the accurate transmission of the law. But now that Moses is gone, our relationship to God must be directly with God.

May the neshama of

בן ציון ראובן
בן ברינה

have an aliyah.
He dedicated his life
to building bridges.